SOLDIERS OF THE PROPHET

SOLDIERS OF THE PROPHET

BY
LIEUTENANT-COLONEL C. C. R. MURPHY

The Naval & Military Press Ltd

published in association with

FIREPOWER
The Royal Artillery Museum
Woolwich

Published by
The Naval & Military Press Ltd
Unit 10 Ridgewood Industrial Park,
Uckfield, East Sussex,
TN22 5QE England
Tel: +44 (0) 1825 749494
Fax: +44 (0) 1825 765701
www.naval–military-press.com

in association with

FIREPOWER
The Royal Artillery Museum, Woolwich
www.firepower.org.uk

The Naval & Military
Press

MILITARY HISTORY AT YOUR
FINGERTIPS

... a unique and expanding series of reference works

Working in collaboration with the foremost
regiments and institutions, as well as acknowledged
experts in their field, N&MP have assembled a
formidable array of titles including technologically
advanced CD-ROMs and facsimile reprints of
impossible-to-find rarities.

*In reprinting in facsimile from the original, any imperfections are inevitably reproduced
and the quality may fall short of modern type and cartographic standards.*

Printed and bound by Antony Rowe Ltd, Eastbourne

يقال   للحِكَم فى الهند * والكِبر فى الفُرس *
وقِرَى الاضياف والشِجاعة فى العرب *
والصدق فى الحبشة * والبسالة والاقدام فى التُرك والاكراد *
وللخيانة فى الأرمن * وللجهل فى الشام * والعلم فى العراق *
والحساب فى قبط مصر * وللحمق فى الطويل *
والكذب فى القصير * وللحفظ فى العميان *
وسوء للخُلق فى العرجان * والعجلة فى الصبيان *
والمِراء فى العلماء * وللحرص فى المشايخ *
والذل فى الايتام * والسلامة فى العزلة *
والصحة فى الحمية *

IT is said that there is wisdom in India; pride in Persia;
hospitality and bravery amongst the Arabs; truth in Abyssinia;
heroism and dash amongst the Turks and Kurds; treachery
amongst the Armenians; ignorance in Damascus; knowledge in
Irak; arithmetic amongst the Copts of Egypt; stupidity in the
tall; lying in the short; memory in the blind; ill-nature in the
lame; haste in boys; hypocrisy in the learned; greediness in
the old; meekness in orphans; peace in solitude; and health
in abstinence.—*A common saying in Damascus.*

NOTICE

CHAPTERS VII., XII., and XIII. appeared in the *Journal of the Royal United Service Institution.* The greater part of Chapters I., II., V., VI., VIII., and X. appeared in the *Journal of the United Service Institution of India.* I have to thank the editors of these journals for giving me permission to reprint my contributions to them ; the editor of the *Journal of the Royal Geographical Society,* for permission to reprint the contents of a letter of mine which appeared in that publication ; the editors of the *Englishman* and the *Pioneer,* for the use of articles from those newspapers ; and the editor of the *Suffolk Regimental Gazette,* for allowing me to reproduce articles contributed to that paper.

ARMY AND NAVY CLUB,
    PALL MALL,
      15*th August* 1921.

CONTENTS

SOLDIERS OF THE PROPHET

CHAPTER I

THE TURKISH EXPEDITION INTO THE HAURAN IN 1910

FOR many years before the military expedition under review the attitude of the Druses towards the Turkish Government had been one of non-co-operation and passive resistance. They were convinced that any acknowledgment of Turkish supremacy on their part would lead to the surrender of their independence and liberty, and therefore they stubbornly resisted all the attempts of the Sublime Porte to subjugate them. They declared that, as they were neither Turks nor Muslims, they would have nothing to do with the Bab-al-'Ali or the Khilafat. All along they had persistently refused to pay taxes. The political movement which had convulsed Constantinople in 1908 had not stirred them. They even repudiated the conscription law which the Constitution had decreed should in future be extended to non-Muslims. As for the alluring promises of the Young Turks that henceforth all Ottoman subjects, of whatever creed or clan, should live together as brothers under the same blue sky, all these had left them stone cold.

The home of the Druses is the Bashan of the Bible; it is now known as the Hauran, and is a district lying to the east of the Sea of Galilee.   At the northern end of it there is a triangular patch of country, of extraordinary volcanic formation, which presents the appearance of a lake of lava which had suddenly congealed whilst in a state of violent ebullition.   The craters are no longer active, but they are numerous and trap-like, and the shepherds are obliged to build sangars round them to prevent their sheep from falling in.   This part of the country, which is known as the Leja, and from which the Druses have expelled the invading Turk on more than one occasion, is an ideal theatre for guerilla warfare.   There is very little water or fuel, and the ground is impracticable for any arm but infantry, so that the difficulties of manœuvre, supply, transport, and operations generally, are very great.   To the eastward lie the wild Druse mountains, and to the west and south the fertile plains which provide the Hauran with rich pasturages.   The villages are built of a dark, basaltic stone which lends them a sombre, almost dismal, appearance.   The houses are often very massive for their size, and, strangely enough, many of them are built entirely of stone, no wood at all being used in their construction.

The mysterious religion of the Druses, which has all along been a contributing factor in their strained relations with the Turks, is a coalescence of unitarianism with freemasonry, perhaps rather more richly embroidered by custom and superstition than is the case with some religions.   On the other hand, the Syrian Muslims constitute a bigoted and fanatical section of the followers of the Prophet.   In 1860, it will be recalled, more than five thousand Christians were massacred in Damascus at their hands.   On that occasion, strange to relate, the Druses sided with the Muhammadans and actually joined in the massacre.   I have spoken to many old inhabitants of Damascus who remembered this tragedy only too clearly. They would tell you that it was precipitated by the wild tales of the Indian Mutiny, which came across the desert from Baghdad with the caravans.   By 1910, the feeling between Muhammadan and Christian had not improved, whilst that between the Druses and their Muslim neighbours had become worse.   Then again, the territory of the Hauran Druses abuts the Syrian pilgrim route to Mecca, and the bitter herbs of hatred are kept green by the Islamic stream which every year, so the Druses imagine, threatens to wash them away, root and branch.

The lawless independence of the Druses and the religious intolerance of their neighbours had more than once resulted in bloodshed, but to get to the bottom of the 1910 trouble one would have to go back two hundred years.   Matters were brought to a crisis in the summer of 1910, when a number of Hauran Druses raided a neighbouring village and killed about fifty Muhammadans.   The raid was said to have been attributable to two influential Muslim families, who lived in the locality and had been stirring up bad feeling against the Druses. The Turks immediately resolved to punish the Druses for this outrage ; their subjection was in every way desirable.   It would bring money into Turkish pockets and good recruits into the Turkish Army, and a successful show of force among the none too loyal peoples of the loose Ottoman confederacy would tend to stablise the Constitution.

Shefket Pasha at once decided to send a large military expedition into the Hauran.   Of the operations which resulted, no official account was published, and only the most meagre and inaccurate details ever found their way into the world's newspapers. It has been said that the Turks make a good deal of history, but do not write it ; nor do they like other people to do it for them. The Englishman says, " Do right, and fear nought " ; the Turk says, " Don't write, and fear nought."

Although the compiler of the following account was in Damascus throughout the whole of the operations, except for one brief visit to the Turkish base at Dera'a, really amazing difficulty was encountered in obtaining information. This was due to the fact that the British officer was no longer welcome in the Turkish Empire, while the Germans, who were already in high favour, strongly resented his presence. Nevertheless, several of these suspected personages found their way to the ancient city in 1910. In August of that year Captain F. E. Packe, of the Welsh Regiment, and Captain G. E. Leachman, of the Royal Sussex Regiment, arrived. They were followed by Captain S. F. Newcombe, R.E. ; and at the beginning of November, two officers of the Egyptian Army—namely, Major C. H. Leveson, 18th Hussars, and Captain G. P. Knott, A.V.C.— came over and bought up a lot of ponies, greatly to the disgust of the German cavalry instructor in Damascus. As I was a resident of the city, I had an opportunity of hearing some of the comments which this influx of British visitors excited.

My information regarding the Hauran was gleaned from such various sources as the following :—General Sami Pasha, the Commander-in-Chief of the expeditionary force ; Field-Marshal

Fetki Pasha, commanding the 5th Army Corps, and the senior military authority in Damascus ; Captain von Hochwaechter, a German officer, who was one of the cavalry instructors to the Turkish Army ; the Bishop of Hauran ; the various consuls in Damascus ; and a host of others, including some of the Druses and *nefers* (private soldiers) who took part in the actual fighting.

The concentration of troops for the Hauran expedition began early in August 1910, and occupied several weeks. The point selected for this purpose was the important railway junction of Dera'a, where the Haifa branch joins the main Hejaz line to Medina—a distance from Damascus of 1303 kilometres. Some of the troops were railed from Aleppo to Damascus, whilst others were sent by sea to Haifa, and at these two termini they were entrained for Dera'a. About 20th September a battalion was pushed up to Bosra Eski Sham, but the work of mobilisation had proved so laborious that a general advance could not be made till the end of that month. Sami Pasha, who had been sent from Constantinople to take command of the expedition, arrived in Damascus during the third week in August, and, in the course of an interview which he accorded me there on 26th August, he informed me that he intended to commence operations, if possible, within a month from that date.

The entire force under Sami Pasha at Dera'a probably did not exceed 21,000 men, and consisted of infantry (mainly Redif, *i.e.* reserve) from the 5th and 1st Army Corps, a few batteries of Q.F. field-guns, a proportion of mountain-guns, and part of a regiment of cavalry from the 5th A.C. in Damascus. On paper, the Fifth Ordu boasted a cavalry division, but actually they could hardly put a regiment into the field.   Most of the infantry battalions possessed a machine-gun or two, and a certain number of men in each *tabur* (*i.e.* battalion) carried hand-grenades.   Communication was kept up by means of field telegraph and telephones. The whole force was organised in two divisions and an independent brigade, and on 19th September the dispositions were as follows :— General Sami Pasha and the Headquarter Staff, and the 1st Division, under Colonel Abdul Hamid Bey, at Dera'a ; the 2nd Division, under Colonel Ali Bey, at Kharabat-al-Ghazala ; the independent brigade, under Colonel Naji Bey, holding a line of villages west of Soueda and Shuhba.

It was almost the end of September by the time Sami Pasha's army had risen up from the yellow plains of Dera'a and penetrated the dark-coloured settlements of the Hauran.   The two divisions headed for the villages of Al-Musifreh and Sikaka, whilst the independent brigade engaged itself in trying to straddle as many of the roads as possible leading out of the Hauran, between the Leja and the Hejaz railway, into Damascus, where the Druses had large numbers of friends and supporters. About this time considerable indignation was aroused in that city by the report that Yahya Atrash, the most powerful Druse chief, together with five of his companions, all of whom had come in with the Bishop of Hauran on 21st September as emissaries of peace to confer with Sami Pasha, had been detained as prisoners.   The Bishop of Hauran informed me that he did not consider that by this act Sami Pasha had abused the privileges of war ; but the Syrians regarded the affair as yet another addition to the scarlet record of Turkish crime, and remarked hopelessly that

" one hole, more or less, in a strainer does not make any difference."

Yahya Atrash certainly seems to have received kind treatment at the hands of Sami Pasha. The following announcement appeared in the *Standard* of 23rd September : " Yahya Atrash, the chief of the rebellious Druses, has surrendered unconditionally with two companions to Sami Pasha. Several other chiefs came in yesterday." That, however, was not the version of the affair that one heard in Damascus.

On the night of 30th September we saw fires burning all along the range of the Druse mountains. The interpretation put upon this in the Damascus *sooks* (*i.e.* bazaars) was that negotiations had failed and that the Druses meant to fight. At that time the 1st Division was occupying the villages of Safah and Hadeed, and the Red Hill—all three of which places are to the east of Soueda ; whilst the 2nd Division was encamped round the dilapidated barracks in Soueda itself. Here the two divisions were split up into three columns, the first of which moved off northwards by way of Kanawat under the command of Badr Khan Bey ; the second, southwards towards Al Kafr ; whilst the third remained behind in Soueda, holding itself in readiness to act in any manner which future developments might indicate. As Badr Khan Bey's column was approaching Kanawat the Druses opened a heavy fire on the Turks, but shortly retired to the neighbouring village of Mafala, where they were able to conceal themselves behind the low walls of the vineyards, and amongst the ridges and groves overlooking the road along which the Government troops were advancing. The rebels were again dislodged without much difficulty,

but fighting of a desultory description continued
for three days. On 1st October Sami Pasha, who
had now moved his headquarters from Dera'a to
Soueda, occupied the villages of Kanawat, Sarkhad,
Atil, and 'Ain Sa'ad ; but only at the first-named
was there any fighting to speak of. At the same
time the Druses, on learning that Dera'a had been
denuded of all its troops except one battalion,
attacked that post and succeeded in cutting the
lines of communication with Damascus. Sami
Pasha, however, contrived to get a message through
to the Mushir, who despatched a battalion to his aid,
and at the same time a small column hurried south
from Soueda, with the result that the Druses were
driven off and two of Yahya Atrash's relatives were
killed. On 3rd October the first convoy of wounded
arrived in Damascus. It was reported that during
the fighting round Kanawat the rebels were joined
by some of the Druses from north Mekran and the
Wadi Liwa. On 8th October the column which was
under the command of Shevket Bey joined that of
Badr Khan Bey and marched to Mardak, where
the 2nd Division had arrived from south Mekran.
Sami Pasha, who was also there, then made Mardak
his headquarters. Reports now kept on coming
in that the rebels were collecting in Shuhba in
large numbers, and it was confidently expected
that there would be a big fight between there and
Al Kanawat. On the 9th October the Mushir told
us in Damascus that he was hourly expecting news
of an important engagement from that quarter.
However, when the cavalry, which had been sent
there to reconnoitre returned, they reported the
village empty ; and so, after all, it was occupied
without resistance. Two days later Badr Khan
Bey's column advanced along the Shuhba road

to Umm-ez-Zeitun ; and on 11th October this column and that of Naji Bey, which had come down the Liwa valley road from Baraq, occupied Matuna without meeting with any opposition.

Let us now return to the 2nd Division, under the command of Abdul Hamid Bey. On 1st October this force advanced on Al Kafr by way of the villages of Imsad-ar-Raha and Sahwat-al-Bilat, a *tabur* being dropped at the latter village to collect arms, but they only succeeded in getting hold of fourteen. So far, none of the rebels had been met with ; but as the remainder of the column were passing through the groves between there and Al Kafr, the Druses opened a heavy fire on them. The troops advanced, the main body heading straight for Al Kafr ; but it took them two hours to clear the Druses out of the vineyards and to effect an entrance into the town. The rebels then withdrew to the surrounding hills and kept up a desultory fire on Al Kafr until sunset. By the next day the force had been divided into two bodies, the first of which went to Habran, and the second into the hills to the south of Al Kafr, one of which is now known as " The hill of Amr Bey " because of a certain Turkish officer of that name who was killed there.[1] That night the Druses attacked Amr Bey Hill, advancing to within " a hundred metres of the Turkish troops "; and at the same time they reoccupied Al Kafr, from which the latter had withdrawn. During this night-attack the various units of the Turkish force repeatedly fired on one another, and yet they had very few casualties. On 2nd October the Druses had to be driven out of Al Kafr for the second time. During

[1] Yuzbashi (Captain) Amr Bey, No. 2 Company, 4th Battalion, 5th Regiment, 1st A.C.

2

the next three days Abdul Hamid Bey was busily
engaged in following them up ; and on 6th October
he entered Soueda. From here he went on to
Kanawat and thence to Mardak, where he remained from 9th October to 22nd October enrolling
conscripts and collecting arms. The columns of
Badr Khan Bey and Naji Bey, which had reached
the villages of Umm-ez-Zeitun and Matuna on
10th and 11th October respectively, received orders
to proceed immediately to the Leja, where the
rebels were reported to have fortified themselves.
According to the leading Damascus newspaper,
Al Muqtabas, a cordon of troops was now thrown
round the Leja, surrounding it "as a bracelet
surrounds the arm"; and detached posts were
established in all the villages from Umm-ez-Zeitun
to Baraq in the Liwa Valley. Then Naji Bey with
a small force marched through the villages of
Ahara, Bosra Hariri, Azra, and Hamar, after
which he left the major portion of his troops in the
Liwa Valley. Numbers of rebels now commenced
giving themselves up, thus facilitating the work of
disarmament and the enrolment of conscripts.
Amongst those who came in was one Yahya Amar,
a rebel chief, who with some of his companions was
detained by the Turks. On 21st October Naji Bey
sent three *taburs* under Lieutenant-Colonel Said
Bey to scour the country between Hamar and
Matuna. It was announced in the newspapers at
this juncture that Sheikh Sad-ud-din Abu Suleiman
with about 200 horsemen came in to offer his
obedience to Sami Pasha ; but, having regard to
the entire absence of sympathy between the Arab
and the Turk, I have no doubt that this report was
an official concoction. The Sublime Porte, for
obvious reasons, always endeavours to conceal the

bad feeling which exists between the Arabs and their co-religionists the Turks.

All fighting being now at an end, the expeditionary force was split up into six columns to complete the work of enrolling conscripts and collecting arms. On 22nd October Sami Pasha returned to Soueda from Mardak, and by the end of the month 350 of the new conscripts were sent from the Sarkhad district to Dera'a by the way of Bosra Eski Sham. A similar number were sent from Soueda to Ahara *via* Kharabat-al-Ghazala ; whilst about 70 more were collected from the district of Ahara itself. With the rounding up of the conscripts in Bosra Eski Sham and neighbourhood, and in the Jebel-ed-Druse, and a further general wresting of arms, the task of the expedition was brought to a conclusion.

As regards the casualties which occurred during this short expedition, it is very difficult to form an accurate estimate. Sami Pasha himself puts his at 93 killed and wounded, and those of the Druses at between four and five hundred. The Bishop of Hauran, who knows the Druses thoroughly well and whose opinion is certainly entitled to great weight, assessed the Turkish losses at 60 killed, and those of the Druses at less than four hundred. He also assured me that, although the fighting strength of the Druses was probably as great as 15,000 men, yet not much more than 2000 actually took the field. The feeble resistance offered by the Druses came as a great surprise to everyone in Damascus, where it was confidently expected that they would show stubborn fight, as they did in September 1896, when they defeated General Abdulla Pasha near Ezra.

From what has preceded, it will be seen that, with

the exception of the two engagements at Kanawat
and Al Kafr, which took place at the very outset
of the expedition, there was practically no fighting
at all, and that after these two defeats the Druses
made no further stand.   Most of the casualties
occurred in Abdul Hamid's Division.   By the close
of the expedition the Druses had handed in perhaps
70 per cent. of their arms.   This, however, could
but paralyse them temporarily, for, as one of them
himself told me, they could get as many rifles as
they liked by sending caravans for them across the
shol (*i.e.* desert) to the neighbourhood of Kuwait on
the Persian Gulf.   For the time being, at all events,
the Druses had bowed to the will of the conqueror ;
but they had been dragooned into submission and
were only crouching in order to spring again.
When I left Damascus in February 1911, it was
the intention of the Turkish Government to leave
a miniature army of occupation in the Hauran, to
consist of 4000 men, of whom 3000 were to be
mounted on mules and the remainder on camels.
The place selected for the headquarters of the force
was Bosra Eski Sham.   They had also announced
their intention of rebuilding the barracks in Soueda,
and of repairing the roads in the Hauran, which
are extremely bad.   A line of outposts was to be
established along the eastern boundary of the
province, beyond the Jebel-ed-Druse, where a chain
of Roman forts once existed.

As regards the results of the expedition, it is
difficult to say whether or not anything of a permanent nature was achieved.   However ephemeral
the success, the Druses had submitted to the Turks.
They promised to pay their share of taxes, and to
furnish a due proportion of young men for the
Imperial Army ; but a promise was a fluid thing

even in those days. Fourteen hundred recruits, as
well as vast quantities of grain, sheep, and cattle,
were taken from them, and, as previously stated,
they were to a great extent disarmed. Several of
the ringleaders were hanged, and the properties
of all those implicated were either confiscated or
destroyed. As a display of force to the disunited
peoples of Turkey in Asia it certainly had the effect
of raising the prestige of the *Doli* [1]—the name by
which the Damascene usually referred to the
Government of the *Bab-al-'Ali.* The Hauran Expedition was the first occasion on which non-Moslem
Nizam (regular) troops were employed by the
Turks. That these only consisted of a mere
handful of Christians is true ; but the extensive
enrolment of Druses at the close of the operations
marked a very important development in this
direction. Sami Pasha had no Syrians under him.

If the rebellion in the Hauran was only quelled
temporarily, nevertheless to Sami Pasha belonged
the honour of having driven it under the surface
even for a time. The general opinion in Damascus
was that he had conducted the expedition with
both firmness and fairness. Undoubtedly his
fluent knowledge of Arabic—a rare qualification
amongst Turkish officials—proved of great value
in dealing with the situation. It is instructive
to notice that out of the conduct of operations in
the Hauran there arose a quarrel between the Wali
of Damascus and the Commander-in-Chief of the
field force ; that is to say, between the civil and
military authorities—a situation not without pre-
cedent in older civilisations. The quarrel ended
in the dismissal of the Wali. Nor was Sami Pasha

---

[1] A corruption of دَوْلَه.

unmindful of the popular aspect of the expedition. He endeavoured to make it as far as possible a demonstration of force, so that it might be an object-lesson to the whole Ottoman Empire. He took care that the arms captured from the Druses should be paraded through the streets of Damascus, and accordingly strings of camels laden with rifles were occasionally to be seen being led through the narrow bazaars with almost comical ostentation. He issued proclamations of the most approved style, and he arranged that the return of the first batches of troops from the Hauran should synchronise with the departure of the Hajj from Damascus—a very important function. In 1910 the *mahmal* did not leave Damascus till the 7th November.

During the fourteen years that had elapsed since the disastrous campaign of Abdulla Pasha, a vast change had come over the Turkish Army. Under Sultan Abdul Hamid the imperial troops outside Constantinople were a half-starved, half-naked rabble ; but since the *Dastur*, as the new constitutional Government is called, the state of the army has improved beyond recognition. I had opportunities of seeing large numbers of Turkish troops, both regular and reserve, on their way to, and returning from, the Hauran ; and they appeared to be thick-set, sturdy men, well clothed and well armed, but poorly shod. The *Redif* troops of which the major portion of the expeditionary force was composed seemed to be in every way superior to the *Nizam* troops, who apparently never got beyond the stage of partly trained recruits. Their drill, which was on German lines, was extremely slovenly, and the general turn-out of the men on parade was bad. As regards musketry they were practically unexercised. The Field Force adopted the head-dress of the Arabs, namely, the *kafiyeh* and the *aghal*, and the men carried bandoliers. Most of the rifles that I saw were in fairly good condition, though some of them showed signs of having been cleaned with hard substances, such as emery, both inside and out. Turkish rifles never become shot out, nor do they often become cleaned out, like so many of our rifles do. The men were well clad in khaki serge, with putties. In the field they were well fed, meat being issued to them three times a week, with a plentiful supply of vegetables, and wheaten bread daily. The expedition was equipped with heliographs, but their signalling results were very poor, and the field telephones which had been served out to them proved absolutely useless, as they were unable to work them. Pack animals, such as camels, mules, ponies, and donkeys, were used for transport, and for the first time in the military history of the Turkish nation, *sukhra*[1] was unknown. The transport arrangements were, however, of a makeshift description, the work being merely muddled through, and it is probable that the Turkish Transport Officer, " seeking that bubble reputation even at the camel's mouth," would find more scope for his abilities under the banner of the Star and Crescent than under any other. But it was perhaps in matters appertaining to sanitation in general, and to water-supply in particular, that the Turks showed the greatest progress. In the campaign of 1896, literally hundreds of their men died of dysentery, and no attempt whatever was made to cope with the disease. During the 1910 expedition, on the other hand, the health of the troops was excellent throughout.

[1] *Sukhra* is forced labour without payment.

CHAPTER II

THE ARAB REVOLT IN KERAK

No sooner had the Turkish Expedition into the Hauran been brought to a conclusion than the Young Turks began to turn their attention further southwards in the direction of Kerak. A reference to a map of Syria and Palestine shows that ancient Moabite capital as lying about midway between the Hejaz railway and the south-eastern shores of the Dead Sea. From time to time numbers of European travellers have visited Kerak, though remarkably few have penetrated into the inhospitable wilds which stretch away from the Dead Sea towards Jauf. To anyone standing on the Mount of Olives in Jerusalem and looking down over the shining levels of the Dead Sea, the high ground immediately above Kerak is plainly visible, though the town itself is hidden from view. The physical geography of this wonderful country forms an interesting study, for here we have a river which close to its source flows through a lake 682 feet below sea-level, and finally empties itself into another lake which is no less than 1300 feet below that level. By a strange coincidence the latter figures also represent the depth of the Dead Sea.

Towards the close of November 1910, the Sublime Porte, acting directly on the advice of the then Wali of Damascus, sanctioned the despatch of a small force to Kerak to strengthen the garrison of that town whilst the new orders regarding disarmament and the enrolling of conscripts were being carried out. The troops selected for this purpose had formed part of the Hauran Expeditionary Force, which was just then being broken up. The work of disarmament and conscription had been so easily and successfully accomplished amongst the Druses that the Wali of Damascus had no difficulty in persuading the central Government to adopt a similar procedure with regard to the district of Kerak. To the Young Turk the project was of course an attractive one, and appealed to his frothy pretentiousness most strongly ; but Sami Pasha, who had commanded the expedition against the Druses, and was himself an Arab, knew that the Government were not strong enough to enforce such measures on the Kerak Arabs, and he accordingly declared himself entirely opposed to the scheme. However, in spite of this warning, the additional troops were sent to Kerak, the intentions of the Government were duly communicated to the sheikhs of Kerak, and their co-operation invited. The news spread like wildfire amongst the neighbouring tribes, with a result which caused some consternation in official circles in Constantinople.

The Commandant of Kerak, little dreaming of the trouble that was brewing, summoned the sheikhs of Kerak to a conference to decide how the orders of Government could best be carried out. The sheikhs said that a strong girdle of posts ought to be thrown round the town, which would have the effect of impressing the tribes with the might and power of the Government. This was accordingly done, and by the 4th December sixteen posts had been established round the town, each consisting of 2 guns and 40 rifles, the remainder of the troops being left behind in the citadel. This, however, was but the kiss of Caiaphas ; for the whole garrison only consisted of two *taburs*, so that the sheikhs had contrived to get the bulk of the infantry, and nearly all the guns, scattered about outside the town. Suddenly at sundown on the 4th December, without the slightest warning, the Kerakis began firing on the Turkish soldiers. Hordes of Arabs came swarming into the town from every direction, and in an incredibly short time were to be seen thronging the streets and running along the roofs of the houses, shooting down every Turkish soldier or Turkish official they could find. A scene of indescribable con-fusion followed. All the men in the detached posts were quickly cut down, with the exception of two in each post who were forced at the point of the knife to lay their guns on the citadel, where their less unfortunate comrades were now surrounded. The Arabs then looted the treasury and the *sooks* (*i.e.* bazaars), making off with three thousand five hundred Turkish pounds, which they got out of the Government chests, and a large sum of Regie tobacco-money besides. No sooner was the pillaging of Kerak completed than the Arabs fled across to the Hejaz railway, where they created the most astounding havoc, com-pletely wrecking the railway stations of Lubin, Jizeh, Qatraneh, and Al-Hassa, and damaging seven others. They broke all the telegraph in-struments, cut down the poles, tore up great lengths of rails at intervals for more than eighty miles, killed several railway officials, and then held up a train, which they looted and afterwards burnt. At the end of four days they disappeared as quickly as they had collected, having killed altogether about eight hundred Turkish soldiers and a considerable number of Turkish officials. The damage to the Hejaz line alone amounted to £100,000, but the total loss to the railway funds must have been vastly greater owing to the stoppage of traffic and the consequent falling-off in returns. Nor was this all ; for the pilgrims who had left Damascus early in November, and who were still in Mecca, were unable to return to their homes by the Hejaz railway, and thousands of them had to make their way to Jeddah and go back by sea instead. So much for the Arab veneration of the *Hajj*.

The discomfiting news of the Kerak revolt soon reached the ears of the Government in Constantinople, who strove by every means in their power to conceal the true facts of the case. And well they might, for the whole Ottoman Empire was now on the verge of collapse. The situation in European Turkey was almost critical ; the outbreak in the Hauran had been but temporarily driven under the surface ; a disturbance was threatening in the vilayet of Baghdad ; desperate trouble was brewing in the Yemen ; there was but a momentary lull on the Russian and Persian frontiers ; and now the storm-centre had shifted to Kerak. While that revolt was taking place, an Arab came round to my house in Damascus and told me a story which made a good allegory on the state of the Turkish Empire at that time. Unfortunately translation mars its brevity and neatness.

There was once a merchant who lived in Damascus. His house was newly built, but it was very rickety and creaked when the wind blew. So one day he went to the landlord and complained about it.

" Do not distress yourself," said the landlord. " When the house creaks it means that it is praising God."

" Undoubtedly," said the tenant with mock reverence ; " but I am dreading the moment when it will worship and fall down."

So it was with the jerry-built fabric of the Constitution. It was new, and yet it was creaking. The Young Turks said it was praising God, but the Arabs knew that it was about to prostrate itself. The people in the bazaars were talking loudly about the deep-seated differences of race and language that lay at the bottom of the rising in Kerak. Official reports were therefore circulated to the effect that the Arabs, enraged at the discontinuance of the annual subsidy of £4000 which had hitherto been paid to them for protecting the Hejaz railway, had been incited by the Druses to rise, and had joined them in the raiding of Kerak and the massacre of Keraki Christians. Of course, all this was mere propaganda. The sole causes of the rising were, as we have already seen, the attempt on the part of the Turkish Government to disarm the Kerak Arabs and to introduce compulsory service amongst them. Not a single Druse took part in this rising, nor was it directed against anyone but Turkish soldiers and Turkish officials. It is true that four Christians were killed, namely, two men, one woman, and one child ; but they were accidentally shot in the course of the street fighting. In a country like the Ottoman Empire, where religious law prevails, and where every war against a non-Moslem enemy is a *jihad,* it is natural that one should hear much boasting about the bonds of friendship between the Turks and their co-religionists all over the world. To tell the truth about Kerak would therefore have been a confession of failure, and would have drawn attention at a critical juncture to the fatuous and illusory nature of the Arab devotion to the Khilafat. *Ar-Rawi,* the Damascus *Punch,* might even have been tempted to perpetrate some irreverent joke about the Sublime Porte and the old, dry Sheri (sacred Muhammadan law) and had its licence revoked in consequence.

In the *Muqtabas,* the leading newspaper in Damascus in those days, the whole Kerak episode was dismissed in four lines, of which the following is a translation :—

" Yesterday 150 Bedouin horsemen raided the station of Al-Qatraneh on the Hejaz line. They plundered it and killed the station-master and wounded several persons ; and they continued to hold up the trains by firing at them ; and communications between Amman and Ma'an are cut." In reality these " 150 horsemen " consisted of several thousand Arabs of the following tribes :— Mujelli, the ruling Keraki family ; Hamaideh, Atami, Salaiteh, Hajaiyah, Saidin, Ghawarni, Jawabari, and some others. Neither the Ruwalah nor the Huwaitat, nor the Beni Sakhr, were actively concerned in the rising, although the last-named were entrusted with the guarding of the railway from Jizeh to Qatraneh and had been receiving an annual subsidy in return for their services.

Kerak was not relieved till 14th December, and for ten days the remnants of the garrison were shut up without food or water. Kerak itself is situated on a hemispherical hill. The water-supply is outside the town and comes from a nullah running round the foot of the hill, and about twelve hundred feet below the citadel. After many failures, a permanent garrison was finally established in Kerak in November 1893, but although the Turks had been in occupation for seventeen years they had not made any provision for a water-supply within the town. When General Salah-ud-Din arrived with the relieving force from Dera'a, the first thing he did was to dig up the graves of the former sheikhs of Kerak, and fling their bones to the wind. He then ordered the troops to bury the bodies of their murdered comrades in the empty graves. This act of vengeance greatly enraged the Arabs, and tended to widen the abyss which has always yawned between them and the Turks.

The Sublime Porte could not do much in the way of reprisals. The completion of the Hejaz railway had undoubtedly strengthened the hold of the Ottoman Government upon the independent tribes who range along its northern sections. Many of the great confederacies no longer enjoyed the full measure of their former autonomy ; for though they were unassailable when they retired into the desert, retribution fell upon them when the summer droughts forced them to return. Still, punitive measures against the Arabs of the desert were out of the question.

In the year 1910, there was the equivalent of about six battalions strung out along the Hejaz railway. There were permanent garrisons at Mismiyah, Dera'a, Kerak, Tufela, Tebuk, and Medain Salih, with small detachments at almost every station. Strategically, the line was badly defended, but the central Government considered it undesirable to try and improve it. The Bedouin problem was too vast to tackle, so they cautiously avoided the larger issue, and treated the Kerak revolt as a purely local affair. Batches of Kerakis were carried off to Damascus, where they were cast into dungeons and treated with great brutality. The prisons were already full, owing to the numbers of Druses that had been brought in from the Hauran, and typhus fever soon began to make ravages amongst the inmates. Some were publicly hanged, many died of disease, and about two hundred others, including Yahya Atrash, the Druse chief, were banished to the island of Rhodes.

It is interesting to note that as soon as these Arab tribes had raised the standard of revolt, they appealed to the *British* Government for help. Berlin was the *qibleh* of the Turks, but never of the Arabs, and I have authority for stating that a certain sheikh of one of the tribes involved in the Kerak revolt applied to the British to send them help from Egypt.

CHAPTER III

THE TEMPLE OF BAAL

And on the summit of the pile
The blue-faced ape of Horus sits
And gibbers while the fig-tree splits
The pillars of the peristyle.—*The Sphinx.*

So much for the blue-faced ape ; but there are other varieties, also to be found amongst ruins, which are not content always to sit and gibber. They seem to fall naturally into two classes : those whom the mere sight of a fallen column almost dissolves into tears, and those who are unable to contemplate such things without being seized with a desire to hack their names somewhere upon the venerable pile. Rarely do we find people who can survey an acropolis with appropriate emotions.

Almost every country in the world can boast of ruins, and ruin-gazing is one of the phases of modern life. In Egypt and India there are numbers of dilapidated temples which people drag themselves out to see. In Greece ruins are almost as common as film stars in America. But what ruins in the world can compare with those of Asia Minor and Syria ? Take, for example, the wrecked shrine of the ancient sun-worshippers of Baalbeck. Few indeed are those who visit the temple of Baal and come away disappointed. Its extraordinary massiveness alone makes it unique, whilst its antiquity might well render it sacred. Yet, like many others, the temples there are overscrawled with names, some laboriously chiselled in the face of the pilasters, and others scratched amongst the elegant tracery of a frieze. Every pillar which " the fig-tree splits " seems to provide fresh space for advertisements of this kind. Even the German Emperor caught the infection when he visited Baalbeck and had his name written up in the Temple of Bacchus. That it is elaborately wrought upon a marble tablet is true, but, after all, even that is only an expensive way of scribbling ·on the wall.

Baalbeck is an easy place to get at ; one has only to go to Beyrout and take a train to Baalbeck station. The first part of the journey, which lies across the Lebanon mountains, is interesting enough, and by the time the train reaches Rayyak, where the Damascus and Aleppo lines meet, you are sufficiently hungry to pay a *mejideh* for an indifferent meal without too much bitterness of heart. From this junction there remains but a short run along the Aleppo line to the destination. There is too much to be seen in Baalbeck in one day, and, moreover, the oftener you go into the temples the better you will like them. For good buildings are like good friends or good plays, or anything else that is good, and improve upon acquaintance. You must get to know them ; so pay your coin and go into the ruins, and the next day go back and do the same. Every time you go in you will find something fresh, you will see something you had not noticed before ; and every day the enormous blocks of stone of which these buildings are constructed will seem to you to grow

3

bigger and bigger. By merely sauntering once through these majestic ruins what conception could anyone hope to get of the former grandeur and magnificence of shrines which took hundreds of years, and thousands of hands and brains, to build ?

The actual origin of Baalbeck is unknown. Its history is largely a tangle of myth and legend, a good deal of which is older than the Bible. This much, however, is certain, that its ruins are amongst the most ancient in the world. The Syrians seem to have possessed at Baalbeck a temple dedicated to Baal, the Sun God, from the remotest ages. The name itself means the *town of Baal*. The sun-worship of Syria was very much akin to the fire-worship of Persia.

When the Greeks came to Syria they named Baalbeck *Heliopolis* because of the temple of the sun which they found there, and which the Syrians claimed to have been built by Solomon himself. After the Greeks came the Romans, who began to build the Great Temple shortly after the birth of Christ ; and although the building operations were carried on for over a hundred years they were never quite finished. Perhaps, however, it would be more accurate to say this of the decorative work only, because in other respects the great temple itself was completed. From the ruins of it which remain it is evident that it must have ranked high amongst the wonders of the world. The Germans carried out extensive excavations in Baalbeck about the time of the South African War and possibly from an archæological point of view did good work ; but they carried off, as a reward for their services, a number of specimens of Greek and Roman art for their museums, and the balance of advantage was certainly not on the side of Baalbeck.

It is recorded that in the seventh, and again in the eighth, century Baalbéck was sacked by the Arabs. They appear to have done as much damage to the great temple as its massiveness would permit, eventually turning it into a fortress, the battlements of which are still visible. During the twelfth century, when Baalbeck came under the sway of Saladin, some of the crusaders were imprisoned and then put to death within these walls. The town was completely pillaged by soldiers of the Prophet, under Timur Bey, in 1400 A.D. Some of the magnificent pillars were overturned by different Walis of Damascus merely for the sake of the iron with which the stones were bound together, and to get at the lead round the fixing pins. Much of what the Arabs and Turks had not destroyed was overturned by a great earthquake in 1759, and so in one way and another these splendid shrines have gradually sunk into the state of ruin in which we see them to-day. Verily " the idols are broke in the temple of Baal."

The ruins consist of five main portions, not including the Temple of Venus, where the obscure and obscene worship of the Goddess of Love went on, and which stands apart from the others. The temples are built looking towards the setting sun. At the eastern end there originally existed an immense flight of stone steps leading up to the main entrance, which in turn opened out into a large hexagonal court. This again led into the court of the altar and thence into the Temple of the Sun, so that the rays of the sun when it rose flooded all three courts.

In the court of the altar there was once a Chris-

tian church, and portions of the altar still remain.
To the south of the Temple of the Sun, and close
to it, is the Temple of Bacchus, which, though small
in comparison to the former, is more ornate and in
a much better state of preservation.   The interiors
of all the courts are now heaped up with ruins.
Red granite monoliths, huge blocks of frieze,
portions of lintels, fluted drums, Corinthian capi-
tals, baths, inscribed tablets, fragments of sculpture,
and dumps of stone balls for *ballista* and *catapulta*,
are to be seen lying about in hopeless confusion.
In spite of this, however, there still remains enough
of the original buildings to give one an idea of
their former grandeur, though it would be hard to
picture what the court of the altar must have
looked like when its eighty-four columns of
polished red granite stood sparkling to the sun, or
indeed the Temple of the Sun, with its vast open
court thronging with worshippers, its innumerable
Gods, and its gigantic peristyle of yellow stone.
Of the latter, there were but six columns still
standing in 1910.   Each of these is sixty feet high
and seven feet six inches in diameter, and consists
of three stones only.   The entablature which
crowns these columns is very ornate and is built
in blocks of stone seventeen feet in height.   How
these masses of material, weighing a hundred tons
and more, were raised up to a height of over sixty
feet above the ground is a mystery of which no
sort of explanation is forthcoming.   Is it possible
that as work went on and the building gradually
rose up they kept on covering it up with sand to
the level of the top and then dragged up these
mighty stones on rollers made from the trunks
of trees ?
   In several places amongst the ruins are to be

seen flights of a dozen or more steps all hewn out of a single block of stone. But the chief wonder of Baalbeck lies in the exterior wall, where there are three stones, each thirteen feet by ten feet, and varying in length from sixty-one to sixty-five feet. Fortunately the Germans did not take these away with them. They are not in the foundation of the wall, but have been built into it at a considerable height above the ground. They are, in fact, the largest stones ever used for building purposes, and their size so astounded the Greeks when they went to Baalbeck two thousand years ago that they named the building the Temple of the Three Stones. The smallest of these three stones weighs about six hundred tons, but in a quarry adjoining the temples there is a stone, carefully hewn and shaped, which weighs over a thousand tons. It has not been actually separated from the living rock, but in other respects it is almost ready to be moved. The Syrians call it *The Stone of the Pregnant Woman.* In comparison with such colossal masses the red granite monoliths of the court of the altar are small, though they are twenty-five feet long. But they are remarkable in another way. It is said that there is no stone of this kind nearer than Assouan in Egypt, and they must have been dragged across the desert by some of the wonderful means known to the people of those days. One hears of the magnificence of the Temple of Ephesus, which once graced the hills behind Smyrna, but could it have eclipsed that of the Temple of Baal?

That there should have been builders in those days who were capable of translating into stone such vast conceptions is very remarkable. How they were able to move such enormous blocks of stone and place them in position with such accuracy is a problem that remains unsolved. Indeed one antiquarian, finding himself at a loss for an explanation, declared that Baalbeck must have been inhabited by a race of giants. What is more surprising is this theory actually gained some ground in spite of the fact that recesses have been found in many of the old quarries, where these very ancients used to work, that will only admit a man of ordinary size.

The Syrians are not greatly interested in these, or indeed in any ruins. They prefer to live in the present rather than try and conjure up the vanished past again. They call themselves "the children of shade and water," and they will sit for hours under a tree by the side of a spring in dreamy, listless reverie, enjoying that state of mind which the Turks call *keyef*. If their forefathers were worshippers of the sun, the modern Syrians are certainly worshippers of the shade.

CHAPTER IV

THE OPERATIONS IN TANGISTAN IN 1913

DURING the month of June 1913 the coast of Tangistan, in the Persian Gulf, became the scene of combined naval and military action. In August 1911 a piracy had been committed on a pearling boat from Dibai by a Tangistani dhow carrying a crew of eleven Persian subjects, who massacred eight persons belonging to Dibai and made off with their boat and pearls. It was soon ascertained that the culprits came from the villages of Dilbar and Madumari, in Tangistan. As, however, neither the central government nor the government of Fars were able to take any steps to arrest and punish the offenders or to obtain compensation, the British Government, with whom rests the suppression of piracy in the Persian Gulf waters, took it upon themselves to exact retribution for this outrage.

For some time past the village of Dilbar had been a centre of gun-running. Roughly speaking, it is situated about twenty-two miles from Bushire as the crow flies, in the direction of south-east by south. Madumari lies some five miles to the south of Dilbar. His Majesty's ships *Pelorus*, under the command of Commander P. W. E. Hill, the senior naval officer in the Gulf; *Philomel*, under Commander G. N. Ballard ; and *Sphinx*, under Commander G. J. Todd, having assembled off the coast, a launch and two armed cutters were sent into the Dilbar anchorage on 11th June, with orders not to land but to bring off any dhows they might find afloat. When the cutters got within about four hundred yards of the shore a desultory fire was opened on them by a large party of snipers hidden amongst the sand-dunes. The fire was replied to with a machine-gun, whereupon the Tangistanis fled back into the village. As all the dhows were found to have been hauled up on the beach, the cutters returned to the ships. There were no casualties.

On 14th June the ships concentrated off Madumari, and after a few warning shots had been fired at 2 p.m., and again at 4 p.m., the village was shelled by all three ships at 6 o'clock. It was again shelled at mid-day on the 15th, after which, at about 1 p.m., every available man was landed under cover of the ships' guns to bring off dhows. On nearing the shore persistent sniping was opened from the beach, one of the landing-party being killed and five wounded, but before a landing had been effected the enemy drew off. Fifteen dhows were found hauled up inside a small creek, from which it would have been impossible to launch them without repeated visits. They were therefore either blown up or burnt.

As the landing-party were about to return to the ships, an envoy arrived under a Persian flag with a letter from the customs representatives of Dilbar. The envoy, who turned out to be an Arab from Baghdad, was taken on board. He declared that most of the houses in Madumari had been affected by the bombardments, and that in the day's fighting the enemy had numbered sixty, out of whom forty were Dilbaris.   He further stated that the enemy had had thirty casualties, and that both Dilbar and Madumari had been evacuated. The letter expressed the grief of the Dilbaris at the reprehensible action of their neighbours at Madumari and begged for an interview on behalf of the inhabitants of Dilbar.   In reply, the headman of Dilbar was informed that the recent fighting had placed them beyond the pale of consideration, and consequently that, irrespective of fines in connection with piracy, they would be required, firstly, to sail off to our ships all dhows between Khor Khuvair and Madumari ; and secondly, to pay forthwith a fine of fifty thousand rupees in cash or in rifles and ammunition.   Failing the fulfilment of these terms, Dilbar would be bombarded and all other dhows on their coast destroyed.

No reply having been received to our ultimatum of 15th June, a combined naval and military force was landed near Dilbar on the 22nd June.   The landing-party was over 500 strong and consisted of 20 officers, 125 bluejackets, 45 marines, and 230 men of the 2nd Q.V.O. Rajput Light Infantry, together with machine-gun detachments, boat-keepers, and ammunition and water-carriers.   The force landed in four steam launches, four dhows, and ten rowing boats.   The landing, which was ably conducted by Commander Ballard, R.N., was effected without opposition of any kind and was completed by 6.50 a.m. after a long wade.

The whole party being now ashore, the command devolved upon Lieutenant-Colonel F. A. Smith, 2nd Rajputs, whose men furnished the firing-line and supports, the bluejackets and marines forming the reserve.   At 7.15 a.m. the advance commenced.

Shortly after 8 o'clock the ships opened fire, but after a few shells had been dropped into Dilbar the bombardment had to be abandoned owing to dust haze.   Dilbar was occupied at 9.45 a.m. and found deserted.   In one of the houses the freshly decapitated head of an Arab was found by one of the marines.   While preparations for the demolition of Dilbar were in progress, a party of the enemy opened fire from a ridge, at a range of about 1500 yards, on a double company of the Rajputs, who were covering the village on the eastern side.   The Rajputs, who picked up the range quicker than the enemy, were immediately reinforced by a party of bluejackets and marines under Lieutenant A. Gordon, R.N., of the *Pelorus*.   This force, with the assistance of the Rajput machine-gun detachment under Lieutenant C. D. Noyes, brought such an accurate fire on the enemy that they soon broke and fled, and before eleven o'clock the ridge was in our hands.   On the far side of the ridge a small encampment was found, and a considerable quantity of bhusa and grain was captured and burnt.

During the advance towards this ridge a party of the enemy estimated at about a hundred strong, with numbers of camels, was seen collecting in the village of Gainak, away on our left flank.   Seeing Dilbar in flames, and probably fearing that Gainak would share the same fate, this party had doubtless hurried back to save and carry off as much as they could.   As soon as they knew they had been discovered they fled, hardly waiting to reply to the fire that was being directed against them.   In the meanwhile most of the important houses in Dilbar had been demolished.   While the roofing of some of the huts was being burnt a quantity of ammunition exploded.   Some important letters, which fully established the local connection with the arms traffic, were picked up in the village. After some desultory sniping the retirement was commenced. The force embarked in the boats at 2.45 p.m., and reached the ships about two hours later. While the landing-party was ashore one of the dhows in which we had landed got aground and had to be abandoned. The following morning Lieutenant Ramsay, R.N., went ashore in an armed cutter and succeeded in bringing off this dhow. As the cutter approached the shore four Tangistanis jumped out of the dhow, having already got the mast away. Lieutenant Ramsay immediately opened fire on them and managed to bag one of the party. The bluejackets then sailed off another dhow which they found near the mouth of a small creek south of Dilbar, and returned before noon with two dhows to H.M.S. *Philomel*.

On 24th June the combined force landed again, this time at Khor Khuvair. The boats were unable to get nearer the shore than about 600 yards, which made the landing difficult. Small bodies of the enemy were observed watching the proceedings from a safe distance. A few shots were fired during the day by the covering parties, but as far as could be ascertained only two shots were fired in return. After another long but unavoidable wade, the force embarked in the boats, having hauled out of the creek four dhows and a fishing-boat, all of which were safely brought off to the ships. The heat throughout these operations was intense. Several of the bluejackets and marines were so badly sunburnt about the arms, legs, and neck that all the sick bays were full for two or three days.

CHAPTER V

THE EARLY OPERATIONS IN MESOPOTAMIA

THE advanced brigade of the Mesopotamian expeditionary force left India on the 16th October 1914, under the command of Brigadier-General (now Lieutenant-General Sir Walter) Delamain. The force consisted of the 16th (Poona) Infantry Brigade, and No. 1 Brigade, Indian Mountain Artillery (23rd and 30th Mountain Batteries), which joined the remainder of the force off Jask on the 21st. The regiments comprising the 16th Brigade were : 2nd Battalion Dorset Regiment, 20th Punjabis, 104th Rifles, and 117th Mahrattas.

Brigadier-General Delamain had received instructions to the effect that :

1. The rôle assigned to his force was that of demonstrating at the head of the Persian Gulf.

2. He was to occupy Abadan Island, with the object of—

    (a) Protecting the refineries, tanks, and pipeline belonging to the Anglo-Persian Oil Company ;
    (b) Covering the landing of reinforcements should these be required ;
    (c) Assuring the local Arabs of our support against Turkey.

3. In the event of hostilities with Turkey, the

remainder of the 6th (Poona) Division was being held in readiness to support his force ; in the meantime he was to take such military and political action as he considered feasible to strengthen his position.

4. If possible, he was to occupy Basrah.

The transports carrying Brigadier-General Delamain's force anchored off Manamah, Bahrain Island, on the 23rd October. They were escorted up the Persian Gulf by H.M.S. *Ocean*, which was sunk in the Dardanelles on the 18th March 1915. As the transports were nearing Bahrain a waterspout rose up ahead, of such a size that the whole convoy had to alter course to get out of its way. It was eventually burst by the *Ocean* firing one of her big guns at it.

Bahrain is the name of the whole archipelago as well as of the largest island in it. It is not a British protectorate, though it is under British protection. A striking feature about this group of islands is the lowness and levelness of the land and the shallowness of the environing sea. The whole of this particular portion of the Gulf, with the exception of one channel, is a mass of reefs and shoals ; in fact Bahrain can scarcely be called a port at all. Ships drawing eighteen feet have to anchor nearly three miles out ; and the *Ocean*, which was drawing twenty-seven feet, had to lie fourteen miles out. There are but few interesting points about Bahrain. One is that in Bahrain Island there are a dozen square miles of prehistoric *tumuli* ; another is that the inhabitants of Muharraq, the second largest island in the group, depend for their water-supply upon submarine springs, fresh water being collected in skins at a depth of from two to nine feet below the surface of the sea. Then of course Bahrain is a great centre of pearl-diving, large quantities of pearls being sent annually, *via* India, to Paris, New York, and London. In 1916 the price of pearls went down to about a quarter of what it was before the war. Another very interesting thing is the coin known amongst the Arabs as the *tawilah*, or " long bit " ; it is made of copper and is shaped like a split pin. The *tawilah* belongs to the Carmathian period, and is one of the most ancient current coins in the world.

Shortly after our arrival in Bahrain, some of us were sent to arrest a German named Harling who was the local agent of the firm of Robert Wonckhaus and Company. As we entered his office he was in the act of signing a letter, which turned out to be a report on the strength and composition of Brigadier-General Delamain's force ; it was addressed to the German Consul at Bushire, and a dhow was waiting to take it away. This document concluded with the remark that so far only about 5000 troops had come up the Gulf, but that 10,000 more were shortly coming from India. Amongst his papers we found a copy of an earlier report, also addressed to the German Consul at Bushire, giving accurate details of the force at anchor off Manamah. This first report had been written and copies despatched, both to Bushire and Basrah, within four hours from the time the transports had anchored. In connection with this incident it is interesting to note the rapid rise of the remarkable firm to which Harling belonged. In 1896 Wonckhaus came to Lingah and started business there by buying shells on the beach. Practically his entire possessions at that time consisted of three wooden boxes, which he used to place in a row at night and sleep on. Five years later he moved across to Bahrain, which he made his headquarters, and shortly afterwards he opened a branch at Basrah. In 1906 the first Hamburg-Amerika liner came up the Gulf, and its arrival there was marked by great rejoicings on the part of the Germans. The steamer entered each port with a band playing ; one and all were invited to dinner and entertained with champagne. Wonckhaus was appointed agent to this line. By the time the Great War broke out Robert Wonckhaus & Company had business houses at Basrah, which was their headquarters, Bushire, Bahrain, Lingah, Muhammareh, and Ahwaz. Their agents were well paid, the partners were rich men ; their houses and offices were luxuriously furnished, and every month they used to remit large sums to the Baghdad railway. Everyone wondered where the money came from : it certainly was not all obtained from profits. In eighteen years this romantic shell-collecting business had grown into a vast and widespread enterprise. It is not too much to say that the aims of this firm were firstly political and secondly economic, and that its representatives were all trained intelligence agents.

Before the war Bahrain had neither wireless station nor cable, and was therefore entirely cut off from the rest of the Persian Gulf. To get over this difficulty the *Ocean* was kept at Bahrain and the *Dalhousie* sent across to Bushire to connect with the cable there. It was hoped that by this means we should be able to keep up communication by wireless with both Bushire and Jask, but for some unexplained reason the arrangements entirely broke down. During the first week we were at Bahrain I failed to get a single message *via* Bushire from my informers up the Shatt-al-'Arab, and eventually I had to go across to Bushire and fetch the messages myself.

On 29th October the British Government learnt with surprise and regret that two or three Turkish torpedo-boats had made a wanton attack upon the harbour and town of Odessa ; that Feodosia had also been bombarded by the Turks ; and that some Turkish officers had landed at Novorossisk and had demanded the surrender of that port. Turkey having now become a hostile belligerent, Brigadier-General Delamain's force, which had not disembarked, left Bahrain and sailed for the mouth of the Shatt-al-'Arab. The force arrived at the outer bar on the evening of the 3rd November. I was still in Bushire when the convoy left Manamah, but managed to pick it up at sea near Kharag Island. The place where we anchored on 3rd November was about fifteen miles from Fao Fort. The next two days were spent in sweeping for mines, but without result, and on the evening of the 5th we crossed the outer bar and anchored just outside the inner bar. This bar is the one blemish of the Shatt-al-'Arab waterway. At low tide there is only about thirteen feet of water on it, but at spring tides, with a combination of daylight and high water, a vessel drawing twenty-three feet might plough through with luck.

It will be convenient at this stage to leave the ships at anchor and to review briefly the military situation in Mesopotamia as it was at the outbreak of the Great War.

Owing to the position of Turkey, and to the certainty of her being driven into the arena by Germany, I had sent off one of my gun-running agents from Bushire, at the beginning of September,

to find out what was going on in the Basrah
vilayet. This man was a Pathan; he spoke
Persian well and had once been in an Indian
cavalry regiment. On the pretence of making
inquiries about a *jihad*, which he declared himself
to be anxious to join, he was allowed to ramble
about the various camps and posts for nearly six
weeks. He used to watch the Wonckhaus coterie
journeying up and down the river in the Turkish
gunboat *Marmaris*. This agent got back to
Bushire just before I left that port to pick up the
convoy. The information he had obtained was
excellent and proved to be of great value to
Brigadier-General Delamain.

The distribution of the enemy's forces in Irak
at the outbreak of war was as follows :—

The 12th Army Corps was in northern Irak.
One division of the 13th Army Corps was in
Baghdad ; the other was on the Shatt-al-'Arab at
a place called Baljaniyah, opposite Muhammareh.
This division, namely the 38th, consisted of seven
battalions, of which one really belonged to the
Gallipoli Army Corps and was composed of
Anatolian and European Turks. On receipt of the
order for general mobilisation an attempt was
made to bring these Irak divisions up to war
strength, and numbers of Arabs, armed with
government rifles but untrained, were impressed
into the service as soldiers of the Prophet. In
and around Basrah there were four or five field
batteries and an equal number of mountain
batteries. There were several machine-guns and
a battalion of gendarmes. Irrespective of any
reinforcements which might have been brought
down from Baghdad, there must have been opposed
to us about 5000 men, including some horsemen

4

and about thirty guns. But if Javid Pasha, the commander of the 12th and 13th Army Corps, or Fourth Inspection as it was called, had possessed a little more practical snap there is no reason why the greater part of the Thirteenth Corps should not have been present at Zain, as we shall see. On the other hand, the British force consisted of about 3800 men, with no cavalry and no field artillery, and only two mountain batteries —so that the enemy were numerically stronger than we, and possessed greater gun power.

It was already known to us that the Turks had sunk four ships and two lighters at the lower end of Shamshumiyah Island with a view to blocking the channel. These vessels consisted of the *Ekbatana*, a Hamburg-Amerika liner of 5000 tons ; the *John O'Scott* ; and two small Turkish-owned steamers, *Kalid-ul-Bahr* and *Ja'fari*. The last-named was an old lightship. The Turks made a poor job of this obstruction, and the ships settled down in shoal water, leaving the fairway open. It is said that it would have been an easy matter to have salved the *Ekbatana* had the work been undertaken before the season of high water. However, the river gradually rose and the vessel sank deeper in the mud, and by the end of March a motor-boat could be driven over her. Above Shamshumiyah Island the steamer channel lies towards the Arabian or right bank of the river, but below that island and between it and that of Umm-al-Khasasif, the main stream sets across towards the Persian bank. Between the two islands the steamer channel is comparatively narrow, and it was principally on that account that this place was chosen for the proposed obstruction. The Turkish main concentration was at Baljaniyah, or Balyaniyah as the Turks called it, and the obstruction was commanded by one of their batteries on the river bank. They had two batteries on Shamshumiyah Island and three guns in Umm-ar-Rasas ; and there were 300 men and two guns on the Turco-Persian frontier along the Khaiyin creek. The Turks had infantry posts on the islands of Shamshumiyah and Umm-al-Khasasif, and on the river-bank at Umm-al-Ghuraib and Umm-ar-Ruwais. Down at Fao there was an Arab frontier company of perhaps 50 men, with a battery of four old-pattern field-guns on the foreshore a little to the northward of the fort. This so-called fort was merely a walled enclosure ; it was not defensible, because there were no banquettes or gun platforms : furthermore, it was almost entirely shut in by date palms. The "fort" was begun in 1896, but some of the money allotted for its construction seems to have been expended in other ways. It was commanded by an officer who was styled "Bimbashi of Fao Fort," but he lived in Basrah. As regards ships, the Turkish gunboat *Marmaris* was in the Shatt-al-'Arab, and the British sloop *Espiegle* in the Karun River. None of our ships was in Turkish territorial waters.

In considering the attitude of the more important sheikhs and rulers, it is only necessary to remember that the sheikhs of Muhammareh and Kuwait were and are our allies, and that Bin Sa'ud, the great chieftain of Nejd, was about to make war on Ibn Rashïd, the Amir of Hail, whose leanings were towards the Turks. The Sharif of Mecca, a dignitary of vast influence, had refused to identify himself with the *jihad* which had been proclaimed in Constantinople ; he knew that the

voice from the minaret was that of a German.
Amongst the chiefs hostile to us were Ajaimi-
as-Sa'adun, of the Muntafik confederacy ; and
Ghadhban, of the Bani Lam.   The Bakhtiari Khans
and the Wali of Pusht-i-Kuh had given us assurances of their neutrality, and so far were maintain-
ing a satisfactory attitude.   This is briefly how
matters stood at the time of the rupture of relations with Turkey.

At 6 a.m. on 6th November, H.M.S. *Odin*, Commander C. R. Wason, R.N., with Captain Hayes-
Sadler, R.N., on board, preceded by two small
armed launches, stood in and bombarded the
Turkish battery outside the fort.   One of these
armed launches, *Sirdar-i-Nafte*, was commanded
by Mr Baillie, an engineer belonging to the Anglo-
Persian Oil Company.   The enemy's guns opened
fire at 10.7 a.m. at a range of 5500 yards ; for a
time they were well served and hit the *Odin* twice,
but by the time the sloop had closed to 1700 yards
they ceased fire after being in action barely an
hour and firing about fifteen rounds apiece.   On
the signal being made that the guns had been
silenced, the transports *Umaria* and *Varela* advanced in that order, each towing eight boats full
of troops ;   the armed launch *Mashona* towed
seven boats full of troops ;   and the Royal Navy
launches towed a detachment of marines from
H.M.S. *Ocean*.   Meanwhile the enemy's infantry
fired a few ineffective rounds at a long range and
decamped.   Opposite the telegraph station the
boats were cast off, whereupon they made for
the shore.   Some 600 infantry landed, with a
section of mountain artillery, complete with mules,
and a squad of sappers and miners.   There was
no opposition.   The fort was occupied during the

night, and the following morning the guns on the
foreshore were dismounted and thrown into the
river. Thus easily Fao passed out of the hands
of the Turks. The Bimbashi of Fao Fort was
killed by a shell whilst in the act of mounting his
horse. This was sheer bad luck, as it was probably
his first visit to the place. The enemy casualties
amounted to eight killed and wounded ; there
were none at all in the British force. The Fao
garrison fled, with the news of their own defeat,
to Baljaniyah where the Turkish commander,
enraged at the loss of Fao and the conduct of its
garrison, ordered three of them to be shot " to
encourage the others."

The British telegraph operators at Fao had been
able to keep up communication with Bushire till
about 5 p.m. on 3rd November, but after that it
ceased entirely. On our arrival at Fao we found
all the telegraph instruments smashed and lying
scattered about the office ; the cable too had been
cut. In those days it ran from the telegraph
offices in a west-south-westerly direction up a creek
and then turned southwards into the Khor 'Abdullah ; it did not run straight down the Shatt-al-
'Arab, as was shown on our maps. The first thing
to be done was to locate the cut, and some difficulty
was anticipated in doing so. The enemy, however,
instead of burying the ragged ends, left one of them
sticking up out of the mud. But for this the
telegraph-ship would have had to have gone out
and grappled for the cable, eventually putting on
a new length of perhaps several miles. This would
have been an expensive business, as the cost of the
cable even in those days was £200 a mile. As it was,
the cable was not repaired for some days, and during
that time we had to depend for our communication

with India upon an improvised and unreliable wireless system and upon the land-line between Muhammareh and Bushire which was seldom in working order.

During the bombardment of Fao the *Espiegle*, which had come down to Abadan, was subjected to rifle fire and had two of her crew wounded. While the troops who had been landed at Fao were being reimbarked on the 7th, the general officer commanding with the remaining transports moved up the river till within sight of the refinery at Abadan. On the 8th the river was reconnoitred for a suitable landing-place. A firm, high bank with deep water close up to it was found at Saniyah; the transports were called up and troops began to disembark. The disembarkation continued during the 9th and 10th, being practically complete by the evening of the latter date. Saniyah is the name of a riparian tract belonging to the Sultan of Turkey; roughly speaking, it is simply a section of the date-palm groves fringing the river-bank. The actual point where we disembarked was about two miles above the oil works. Here we made an entrenched camp.

Brigadier-General Delamain's intention was to advance from this camp and attack the Turkish position at Baljaniyah by land, but reports of the movement of enemy forces southward, and the necessity of safeguarding the oil works, combined with the absence of news from India regarding his reinforcements, decided him to remain at Saniyah. In view of the intention of an early forward movement, as little baggage and supplies as possible were landed. Reconnaissances both up and down stream on the 9th and 10th failed to discover any enemy.

It was now over seventeen days since we dropped anchor off Manamah, and we knew that through the good offices of Harling and his consul, Listemann, at Bushire, our movements, as well as the exact composition of our force, had been communicated to Subhi Bey, the Turkish commander at Baljaniyah. Subhi Bey was not looked upon at the Seraskerat as a Yildirim,[1] but at any rate he was a Turk, whereas his troops were mostly riverain Arabs ; and a one-eyed man is a king amongst the blind. Shortly after the capture of Basrah we found a copy of a telegram from Subhi Bey, dated 29th October, forwarding to the Ministry of War in Constantinople the substance of Harling's report from Bahrain on the strength and composition of our force. Javid Pasha had therefore nineteen days in which to transport the 37th Division from Baghdad to Zain, had he cared to do so. The journey would have only occupied about seven days, and there were sufficient steamers and barges at Baghdad at that time to have brought down the bulk of the division.

On the evening of the 10th reliable news was received from a friendly sheikh to the effect that about four hundred Turks under one Sami Bey, with a number of Arabs, intended to attack our camp at Saniyah at dawn on the 11th. At 2.20 a.m. we received another report from the same source saying that the attacking force had started, and that its objective was two mounds near the northwestern edge of our camp. On receipt of this news our troops were turned out and outposts strengthened. At 5.30 a.m., when it was still dark, a single shot was fired. A moment later

[1] The Seraskerat is the Ministry of War, Stamboul ; Yildirim was the nickname of Sultan Bayazid, and means " lightning."

there were half a dozen more shots ; then came a
tremendous fusillade. The Turkish force, of whom
over three hundred were actually seen, delivered
a determined attack on an advanced post held by
a double company of the 117th Mahrattas, with
two machine-guns. They advanced to within
fifty yards of the post, but were driven off by a
dashing counter-attack, delivered by the 20th
Punjabis, with the assistance of the 23rd Mountain
Battery. As the sun rose two large bodies of the
enemy were observed from the crow's nest of the
Espiegle to be advancing across the desert towards
our camp. Soon, however, the firing began to
slacken and these two bodies were seen retiring.
They were the enemy's supports and reserves, but
they had lagged behind and Sami Bey's attack was
smashed before they could render any assistance.
The mountain batteries shelled the enemy as they
retired across the desert, and the *Espiegle* was able
to get a few rounds in at them through gaps in the
palm belt. The Turks under Sami Bey belonged
to the 1st Battalion of the 26th Regiment, which
ordinarily formed part of the 3rd Army Corps
in Gallipoli. Their casualties amounted to eighty
killed and seriously wounded ; they also lost a few
prisoners, one of whom—an Arab—remarked to
the author that " someone must have betrayed
them." Amongst the killed was Sami Bey, their
intrepid leader ; he was a young captain, and was
considered to have a great future before him. Our
casualties were slight, but included Major R.
Ducat, 20th Punjabis, who died of wounds ; and
Captain K. F. Franks, 117th Mahrattas, severely
wounded. The latter was the first British officer
hit in Mesopotamia. In one place we found the
dead bodies of a section of the enemy's infantry,

extended with great precision to three paces. They were excellently equipped and accoutred, and were armed with new Mauser rifles, with long bayonets, and brand new ammunition with pointed bullets. Some of them also carried bombs, but only a few of their men got an opportunity of using them. One or two of their wounded opened fire on our stretcher-bearers whom we had sent out to collect them. The night of the 10th–11th was cold, with some showers ; during that of the 11th–12th there was rain and thunder, but no attack.

This affair at Saniyah marked an important event. It was the first occasion, not only in the Great War, but in the whole of military history, in which British troops have engaged regular Turkish-speaking soldiers of the Ottoman Empire. It is remarkable that the 16th Brigade, to whom this honour fell, should have included the Dorset Regiment, already distinguished as first in India and first in Irak.

After this defeat the enemy took up a position about four miles up the river in a tract called Saihan. It was known that their main concentration was at Baljaniyah, and Brigadier-General Delamain considered it imprudent to attack them at Saihan, situated as it was within striking distance of superior enemy forces. Suddenly, however, we received a massage from Lieutenant-General (now Field-Marshal) Sir Arthur Barrett saying that he had arrived at the mouth of the river and that he had had no word from us since he left India. We then learnt that five transports containing the 17th and 18th Brigades were already at the bar. The composition of these two brigades was as follows :—

17th (Ahmednagar) Brigade—Brigadier-General W. H. Dobbie, C.B.; 1st Battalion Oxford and Bucks L.I., 103rd Mahrattas, and 119th Infantry.

18th (Belgaum) Brigade—Major-General C. I. Fry; 7th Rajputs, 110th Mahrattas, and 120th Rajputana Infantry.

That morning, 4th November, I went off to try and find out something about the disposition and strength of the enemy's troops in the date belt between Shamshumiyah Island and Saniyah. I went down to the oil works and walked across Abadan Island to the Bahmanshir River, where I hired a small native boat and went up to Muhammareh. Here I was able to discard my khaki and put on clothes more suitable to the occasion. I was able to watch the Turks " digging like beavers " and making earthworks at Umm-ar-Rasas. The next morning I rigged myself out as an Arab and started off before daylight with a party of Sheikh Khaz'al's men. We all walked along together down the left bank of the river, talking loudly. We noticed several small parties of the enemy in the date groves opposite ; we could see them clearly and even hear them talking, though it was not possible to distinguish what they said. Soon we heard firing, and by the time we got abreast of Saihan a general action was in progress. We soon learnt that Sir Arthur Barrett had ordered Brigadier-General Delamain to reconnoitre the Turks' advanced position at Saihan and to try and dislodge them without involving his own force too seriously.

The force under his command consisted of the 30th Mountain Battery, the 2nd Battalion Dorset Regiment, and the 104th Rifles, with the 23rd Mountain Battery and the 20th Punjabis in camp held ready to reinforce if he became engaged. The force marched at 6 a.m. from Saniyah, and on reaching the southern edge of the date palms turned westwards, the advanced guard under Major B. St. J. Clarkson, Dorset Regiment, consisting of four companies of the Dorsets and one section of the Mountain Battery, keeping 1200 yards from the edge of the date groves and followed by the main body at about the same distance. The march was continued in this order till the advanced guard was approximately south of Saihan village and creek at 7 a.m. Ten minutes later the enemy opened fire on the advanced guard from two positions on the edge of the date groves with rifles and machine-guns, and on the main body with artillery. The 104th Rifles were sent immediately to turn and capture the enemy's first position and then to work through the date groves from the east. Two sections of the Mountain Battery assisted the 104th Rifles, and the remaining section kept the hostile guns in the Turkish second position in check. The 104th Rifles took the first Turkish position in capital style about 8.30 a.m. At the same hour the reinforcements arrived from camp.

The advanced guard was then reinforced by the remaining half-battalion of the 2nd Dorsets and extended to their left so as to outflank the second Turkish position from the desert side. The 30th Mountain Battery was put under the orders of Lieutenant-Colonel H. L. Rosher, commanding the 2nd Dorset Regiment, who now commanded the advanced guard. The 20th Punjabis (less four companies) filled the gap between the advanced guard and the 104th Rifles on our right, leaving the other four companies of the 20th Punjabis and the 23rd Mountain Battery in reserve under Brigadier-General Delamain's own hand. A general advance was then made on the second Turkish position assisted by the fire—admirably directed—of both mountain batteries, from which the enemy suffered considerably. The position was entrenched and held by the Turks with determination. It was gallantly rushed by the 2nd Battalion Dorset Regiment about 9.30 a.m., whereupon the enemy made off northwards through the date palms.

The arrival of Turkish reinforcements from Baljaniyah was now to be expected at any moment. In view, therefore, of his instructions not to get too seriously engaged, Brigadier-General Delamain ordered a withdrawal to Saniyah after doing considerable damage to the Turkish camp. The retirement was unmolested.

The enemy, who were commanded by a staff officer named Major Adil Bey, sustained casualties to the extent of 250 killed, wounded, and prisoners. Our own casualties were slight and only amounted to 65 killed and wounded, including Captain G. G. C. Maclean, 104th Rifles, and Lieutenant G. D. Yeatman, Dorset Regiment, both severely wounded.

On the morning of 14th November the S.S. *Elephanta,* with General Barrett's headquarters, and four other transports came up the river and anchored opposite Saniyah where the 16th Brigade had been bivouacking since the 8th. The disembarkation of troops was begun at once. The infantry used the ships' boats and were quickly ashore. The landing of the guns, wagons, and horses of the field artillery and the cavalry horses in lighters and dhows was a more difficult matter and was delayed by the strong tide and current, the want of suitable landing-places, and by the shortage of lighters and steam craft for towing purposes. The hatch-covers of the transports were used as ramps for the horses and guns. The only regrettable incident that occurred was that two mules fell overboard in mid-stream. One swam towards the Arab shore and was soon in camp with his friends; the other had evidently been got at by the Germans, for he landed on the opposite bank and violated Persian neutrality.

General Barrett's information on the 16th November was to the effect that a force of the enemy would probably be met with in the Zain tract, their headquarters being at Baljaniyah; there were no large bodies of troops in the date palms along the river's edge. By this time the whole of the cavalry, sappers, and infantry of the 18th Brigade had been landed, but only one battery of the 10th Brigade, R.F.A. General Barrett was aware that the Sheikh of Muhammareh was apprehensive of an attack by the forces of the enemy on the left bank of the river; also that the attitude of the riverain Arabs depended upon our ability to make rapid headway against the Turks. He therefore decided to advance at once with the troops at his disposal, leaving the remaining field batteries to come along after us. His intention was to turn the enemy's right flank and drive them through the palm groves on to the river front so as to give the sloops a chance of co-operating.

The British force, consisting of the 16th and 18th Brigades under Brigadier-General Delamain and Major-General Fry respectively, left Three Bridges, on the south-western face of our entrenched camp at Saniyah, at 6 a.m. on 17th November and moved across the open desert, the surface of which, owing to the recent rain, was still very muddy in places though fortunately free from creeks and other obstructions.   At 8.50 a.m. a report was received from the advanced guard to the effect that the enemy's position extended from an old mud fort, which was now plainly visible somewhat to the right of our line of advance, north-westwards to the white mosque of Mir Abul Hasanain.   This information proved substantially correct, but their line was prolonged southwards from the old fort (Kut-az-Zain) for about 1200 yards along the date-palm belt.   At 10 a.m. the enemy's guns opened fire.   General Barrett then ordered the 110th Mahrattas to reinforce the advanced guard, and moved up the 16th Brigade on its right, retaining as reserves the 48th Pioneers and the 120th Rajputana Infantry.   Each of the two brigade commanders had now at his disposal three battalions of infantry and a company of sappers. The two squadrons of the 33rd Light Cavalry were covering the left flank of the whole force, and the two sloops, *Espiegle* and *Odin*, were on our right, though at some distance, with only the tops of their masts appearing above the date palms.   The whole of the artillery, consisting of the 63rd Battery, R.F.A., subsequently joined by three guns of the 76th Battery which were hurried up during the action from the landing-place, and the 23rd and 30th Mountain Batteries, were placed under the orders of Brigadier-General C. T. Robinson, C.R.A.

While these dispositions were being made a heavy downpour came on and lasted for half an hour.   The front was entirely obscured, while the surface of the ground was converted into a quagmire over which guns and horses could only move at a walk. The enemy's guns ceased firing, and General Barrett began to doubt whether they would maintain their position. Our troops, however, continued to advance steadily ; the sun was now shining again, and at 11.45 a.m. the enemy simultaneously opened a heavy gun, rifle, and machine-gun fire along his whole front. Our artillery and infantry also came into action. After watching the engagement for some time, General Barrett decided to abandon his original intention of turning the enemy's right which extended some distance and was echeloned back into broken ground and palm groves. The kut was evidently the key of the position. He therefore sent word to General Fry with the 18th Brigade to engage the enemy's right and centre with a frontal attack, while General Delamain with the 16th Brigade turned his left and captured the fort. At the same time Sir Arthur Barrett reinforced General Delamain with a battalion from the reserve. General Delamain had meanwhile anticipated the force commander's intentions and had already commenced the turning movement. Almost immediately afterwards Captain R. L. Birdwood, assistant political officer to the force, was hit by a number of shrapnel bullets and instantly killed whilst in the act of speaking to the author ; and Colonel U. W. Evans, R.E., who was also on Sir Arthur's staff, was wounded. It was at this stage that a large number of casualties occurred on our right, especially in the Dorset Regiment, which had been the first to come into action and had met with a very heavy cross fire from the enemy's trenches, the mud fort, and the palm groves. The Turkish regulars were using smokeless powder and were invisible from the point where our guns were in action, the latter being fully engaged with the enemy's artillery and with the long line of entrenchments between the mosque and the kut. The sloops on the river were unable to do more than put three or four shells into the enemy's position, as the thick belt of date palms completely shut out the view. This turning movement was the critical phase of the action; it was skilfully carried out by the 16th Brigade and led by General Delamain, who was one of the first into the fort.

At 1.15 p.m. the whole of the enemy's line rose up, quitting their entrenchments and fleeing across into the broken ground and palm groves. At this moment an extraordinary mirage came on. The long line of grey Turks and motley Arabs suddenly melted away, and in its place was a sheet of rippling water with the enemy, all unsubstantial, shimmering in the air above it. Meanwhile our troops were advancing steadily and keeping up a heavy rifle fire on the enemy as he materialised from the mirage. As there was no telling what the future might hold in store, Brigadier-General Robinson was obliged to exercise the strictest economy in gun ammunition; the batteries were therefore ordered to cease fire. Fortunately too for the enemy the slippery state of the ground precluded rapid movement, especially on the part of the cavalry. But for these two factors the enemy would no doubt have lost most of his guns. As it was, only two mountain guns and about fifty prisoners, including three officers, fell into our hands.

At 2.50 p.m. General Barrett ordered the pursuit to be stopped. The enemy were then retiring through the palm groves, with banks and mud walls affording him facilities for defence. We had to form an entrenched camp before nightfall and to bring in a large number of wounded who were scattered over several square miles of country. Our casualties in killed and wounded during the day amounted to within a dozen of 500, including 21 officers ; those of the enemy in killed, seriously wounded, and prisoners, amounted to about 800, as nearly as can be ascertained. In one section of his trenches we found sixty-nine bodies in a row. The hospitals in Basrah were full of wounded Turks and Arabs for some weeks after its capture. During the night of the 17th–18th our troops bivouacked on the bank of the river ; no attack was made, but there was a good deal of firing at the pickets. The work of bringing in the wounded continued far into the night, and one ambulance party remained out till the next morning. In addition to our own men, a large number of wounded Turks and Arabs received attention.

Scarcely had the enemy's position been captured when one of those winds, well known in the Gulf as a *shamal*, sprang up and blew with some violence for several hours. Three large dhows, which were lying alongside the transports laden with stores ready to be put ashore, were wrecked and ten sepoys and two lascars were drowned. The wind and the strong tide and current made boating operations hazardous, and the result was that none of the wounded were able to be got off to the transports till the morning.

The next three days were spent in landing supplies for the troops and in reconnoitring the enemy's position at Baljaniyah, which was found to be at right angles to the river, with four guns in position on the bank commanding the obstructions already referred to. General Barrett formed a plan of

5

attack on Baljaniyah to be carried out on 22nd
November by the combined naval and military
forces ; but on the 21st he received information
that the enemy had vacated their position and
fled northwards, and that the town of Basrah was
in danger of being looted.   On receipt of this news
General Barrett immediately ordered a forced
march on Basrah.   The troops were to start at
8 p.m. that evening ; the sloops were to go on up
the river and try and get through the obstruction,
and two battalions were hastily got on board
shallow-draught steamers to follow them.   The force
started off at 8 o'clock that night across the desert,
and by noon the next day had reached the outskirts
of Basrah after a march extremely trying to the
troops.   Frequent delays were caused by the water
channels which had either to be bridged, or else
their high banks levelled, to allow of the passage of
field guns.   The two sloops, having got through
the obstruction, reached Basrah at 9 p.m. on the
21st and the two battalions at 9 a.m. on the 22nd.
On the 23rd the troops made a ceremonial march
through the town to a selected spot on the 'Ashar
creek where the foreign consuls and the Basrah
notables were assembled to meet them.   A proclamation prepared by Sir Percy Cox, chief
political officer, was then read, the Union Jack was
hoisted, a salute was fired from the ships, the
troops presented arms, and three cheers were
given for His Majesty the King.   The German
consul and five other Germans were placed on
board transports for conveyance to India.

Early in December a camp was formed at Magil,
about four miles above Basrah, and the 17th
Brigade was sent there.   Magil was a depot for
material for the Baghdad-Basrah railway, and

large quantities of railway stores were found there. At this depot the Germans had made a wharf, and had erected landing cranes and other structures. Just above Magil, at a place called Gurmat 'Ali, the Euphrates enters the Shatt-al-'Arab along its new channel. As soon as Basrah was occupied it became known that the Turks who had fled from the battle-field of Zain were reassembling at Kurna, a small town about fifty miles above Basrah, where some of the waters of the Euphrates still find their way into the Tigris. Kurna is the fabled site of the Garden of Eden. The two rivers here form a great contrast to one another, the Euphrates clear and feeble and the Tigris brown and sturdy. It is curious to note that the Karun and the Shatt-al-'Arab at their junction also form a contrast to one another, though in a different way. If you put your hand into the river opposite the British Consulate at Muhammareh you will find the water much colder than it is a few yards away in the Shatt-al-'Arab, and sometimes there is a difference of as much as sixteen degrees Fahrenheit. The river from Kurna to the sea is called the Shatt-al-'Arab, and has been aptly described as the spacious vestibule into Mesopotamia, the Tigris and Euphrates forming as it were two long corridors into the interior.

On 3rd December a column was sent up the river to deal with the Turks at Kurna. The force originally despatched from Basrah for this purpose consisted of the 104th Rifles and the 110th Mahrattas, one company of the 2nd Norfolks, two guns of the 82nd Battery, R.F.A., and a half company of the 3rd Sappers and Miners, under the command of Lieutenant-Colonel Frazer. Two of the transports containing these troops were armed with two field guns each, which did great execution. The flotilla accompanying the column consisted of the *Espiegle,* the *Odin,* the *Lawrence,* and three armed launches, *Miner, Lewis Pelly,* and *Shaitan.* Early next morning the expedition reached a point about four miles below Kurna, but on the opposite bank, where the troops were landed. The ships did not get much beyond here at first, but the paddle-steamers went ahead and used their field guns with great effect. The armed launches got in still closer and did splendid work. Lieutenant-Colonel Frazer at once made for the village of Mzaira'ah, which was soon taken. The enemy were pursued, but as our troops approached the river bank opposite Kurna, they came under a very heavy fire from across the stream and it soon became evident that Kurna could not be taken by nightfall. The column therefore withdrew to the mouth of the Suwaib creek, about three miles to the south-east of Mzaira'ah, where they bivouacked and entrenched themselves. Just as Lieutenant-Colonel Frazer had given the order to retire, his staff officer, Captain L. H. Branson, was wounded. During the night the Turks were reinforced, so Lieutenant-Colonel Frazer sent word into Basrah for more troops. On 6th December General Fry arrived with more infantry and guns. By this time the Turks had reoccupied Mzaira'ah whence they made an irresolute attempt to advance against our camp. On the morning of the 7th the action of the 4th was fought over again, General Fry's order of battle being as follows :—

Infantry.—2nd Battalion Norfolk Regiment, Lieutenant-Colonel E. C. Peebles ; 7th Rajputs (less one company), Lieutenant-Colonel N. E. Robin ; 104th Rifles, Lieutenant-Colonel C. B.

Clery; 110th Mahratta L.I., Lieutenant-Colonel G. S. Frazer; 120th Rajputana Infantry (less two companies), Lieutenant-Colonel E. Codrington.

Artillery.—76th Battery, R.F.A. (less one section); 82nd Battery, R.F.A., one section being in the *Mejidieh* and another in the *Blosse Lynch*; and the 30th Indian Mountain Battery.

Engineers.—17th Company, 3rd Sappers and Miners (less two sections).

During the action of the 7th the armed launch *Shaitan* was disabled and her gallant commander, Lieutenant-Commander Elkes, of the R.N. Reserve, was killed. Mzaira'ah was taken a second time, the Turkish trenches were cleared, and the survivors withdrew across the river. General Fry's plan for taking Kurna was to cross the Tigris some distance higher up and then to attack from the north and west. Accordingly, early in the morning of the 8th, the 104th and 110th regiments were marched up the river with two mountain guns. Lieutenant M. G. G. Campbell, R.E., and some Muhammadan sappers then swam across the stream carrying a line with them to which a steel hawser was attached. Considering that the Tigris is about 120 yards wide here, and that the enemy were in the vicinity of the landing-place, this was a fine performance. With the aid of a large *mahailah*,[1] which the Turks had kindly left for us, a flying-bridge was constructed, and the two battalions and the guns were got safely across. No attempt was made to take Kurna that night, and so the force bivouacked and entrenched itself, the main portion on the left bank and the remainder on the other.

[1] A high-peaked and sterned boat used in the Shatt-al-'Arab for cargo lightering.

About midnight on the 8th a steamer ablaze with lights was seen coming down stream. She carried three Turkish officers bearing a message of surrender from Subhi Bey, who was commanding the 38th Division, and had been acting Wali of Basrah. General Fry insisted on an unconditional surrender, and so at 1 p.m. the next day the remnants of the Turkish garrison appeared before their trenches and laid down their arms. The Turkish officers then came forward and handed up their swords. General Fry returned Subhi Bey's sword in recognition of his having put up a good fight. The captives numbered 45 officers and 1000 men. Many of the enemy had escaped during the night, and our troops were surprised at the large garrison remaining. Several more guns were taken. The Turkish casualties in and around Kurna and Mzaira'ah were about 500 killed and wounded, ours being roughly a half of that total.

In January a force of some 5000 Turks and Arabs established themselves round the Rotah creek, about six miles up the river above Mzaira'ah, and so on 20th January General Barrett made a reconnaissance in force against them from Mzaira'ah. We drove the enemy's outposts across the creek and shelled his camps and river boats, but we found out absolutely nothing about the enemy's strength or dispositions. Indirectly, however, the day's work had been of value because it proved that in this country of marsh and mirage, of innumerable creeks and obstructed rivers, reconnaissances by land or water are practically useless, and that the only medium for this purpose is aircraft, which we did not possess.

About this time we read in the home papers that the British were now in occupation of the richest part of the Mesopotamian Delta, and that we were being welcomed by the Arabs. As regards their attitude generally, they were genuinely pleased to see the Turks being ejected, but they did not want us or anyone else to take their places. Turkish rule was despotism tempered with assassination, and the Arabs had had enough of it, but they foresaw that in the trail of this storm there would come law and order, and they do not like law and order ; it cuts both ways. The Arab in fact does not wish to own allegiance to anyone, and he reserves to himself the exclusive right to fire on whom he pleases.

The enemy's forces were now disposed in three bodies : his right on the Euphrates, his centre on the Tigris, and his left on the Karun. The rivers were rising rapidly, and the country round Kurna was already under water, absolutely precluding any sort of military operations. General Barrett was of course aware that the Turkish movement against Ahwaz was merely a ruse to make him dissipate his forces, and he was strongly opposed to sending any troops up the Karun at all. He had, however, to choose between detaching a force to the Karun, and abandoning his ally the Sheikh of Muhammareh. The latter course meant allowing the Turks to raid Arabistan unmolested, which would have had a fatal effect on the Sheikh of Muhammareh's already wavering tribesmen as well as on the Bakhtiaris, and might indeed have set the whole country ablaze. Political considerations, therefore, seemed to him to be paramount, and troops were sent to Ahwaz. The hostile forces threatening that town were severely handled by General Robinson on 3rd March, though with some loss to his own side. In this action

Lieutenant-Colonel Parr and Captain Ogg, both 7th Rajputs, and Lieutenant Sheepshanks, 12th Cavalry, distinguished themselves [1]; and a handful of the Dorset Regiment under Lieutenant Baillie rendered splendid service. The situation, however, showed little improvement, and before long it was decided to send more troops into Arabistan. Towards the end of April, General Gorringe's Division left Basrah for the Karun, the cavalry and transport animals marching overland, and the remainder going by river. On the 6th May the division concentrated at Illah, on the Karkhah River, which is here 224 yards broad and 24 feet deep. This crossing was a big business, but was very successfully accomplished. By this time most of the Turks had cleared, and General Gorringe was unable to do more than round up those of the enemy that remained and burn a few villages. He was also able to inflict some punishment on those Arabs who were concerned in the treacherous attack on our cavalry on the 29th April by which three British officers lost their lives. The division, less the bulk of the 12th Brigade which went on to 'Amarah, then returned to the Karun, and reached Basrah about the third week in June. The result of all this was that Arabistan was completely cleared of the Turks, and the Sheikh of Muhammareh's authority restored. More than this, the 142 miles of pipe-line between the oilfields at Maidan-i-Naftun and the refinery at Abadan, about a mile of which had been completely destroyed by fire, were repaired, and from that time crude oil continued to come into Abadan. Some idea of the importance of the Anglo-Persian

---

[1] Also Captains J. W. Roe and G. F. R. Wingate, both of the Royal Field Artillery and on General Robinson's staff.

Oil Company's possessions to the Allies may be gained from the fact that even in those days their refinery was capable of dealing with six or seven millions of gallons of crude oil monthly, and that a great deal of this vast quantity was being made into fuel for the British Government.

During the first week in February 1915 Lord Hardinge of Penshurst, Viceroy and Governor-General of India, came up to Basrah on a visit. It was just at this time that we received the first news of the Turkish concentration which was then in progress at Nasiriyah. Our cavalry from Shaiba began to get into regular touch with the enemy's cavalry, and on 3rd March there was a sharp cavalry engagement. On 16th March a large body of Kurds and Arabs made a determined attack on Shaiba, but were brilliantly repulsed by General Delamain's cavalry and artillery, solidly assisted by the Dorset Regiment. Every day it became clearer that the enemy's main attack was to be delivered by his right wing, and that the Turks had a firm intention of carrying out their threat to retake Basrah. There is not the least doubt that but for their bad intelligence and their inertness the attempt might have been entirely successful. For three months after the capture of Basrah the largest available striking force with which we could have opposed them was four battalions, four squadrons, and ten field guns ; and it was sometimes less. Even up to the middle of March it never exceeded six battalions, and was often less. In the middle of February the enemy had twice as strong a force both in infantry and cavalry, and with equal gun power, at Nakhailah as we had at Basrah and Shaiba, and they were only two days' march from our trenches. They

also had with them the Arab tribesmen under
'Ajaimi and other sheikhs, and another division
was on its way down the Shatt-al-Hai, so that
their reinforcements were closer to hand than ours.
By the time the Turks attacked we had nearly
sixteen battalions in the Basrah area.   Even then,
with all our reinforcements, the enemy succeeded
in completely cutting off Shaiba from Basrah, and
the issue of the battle, as we shall soon see, hung
in the balance for several hours.

The enemy's advanced position on the Euphrates
line was at Nakhailah.   That, they considered,
was the nearest safe point to Basrah at which they
could concentrate against us.   We soon learned
that they were bringing down supplies in *mahailahs*
and collecting them there, so that if necessary they
could make a dash across the desert.   General
Barrett thereupon had two 5-in. guns mounted on
steel barges and sent up the new channel of the
Euphrates from Gurmat 'Ali with orders to try
and get above Nakhailah and so institute a blockade
of that " port."   This Blockade Flotilla did great
damage and made a good bag of *mahailahs* ;   no
doubt it also delayed the enemy's advance.

Time went on, and still the enemy made no
move.   This fatal delay on their part was due to
the fact of Sulaiman Askeri being kept waiting for
his troops ;   more than half of his regular infantry,
besides four field batteries and two mountain guns,
had to be brought down to Nasiriyah from the
Tigris *via* the Shatt-al-Hai, a necessarily slow
operation.   Another retarding force acting upon
him was the Arab tribesmen, whom the Turkish
commander had the greatest difficulty in organis-
ing and marshalling for the attack.   By the end
of March the desert grass, which springs up after

the winter rains, dies down, so that the longer the Turks delayed the greater would be their difficulties. Indeed, horses can scarcely live in the desert for any length of time when once April has set in. It almost looked as though Sulaiman Askeri, like William the Conqueror at Senlac, was trying to tempt the English out of their position.

On the 9th April 1915 General Sir John Nixon, K.C.B., took over command of the Mesopotamian Expeditionary Force from Sir Arthur Barrett, who was granted leave owing to ill-health.

On the 11th April the Shaiba garrison consisted of eight battalions, nine squadrons, one battery R.H.A., and eleven field guns, with two companies of S. and M., the whole being under the command of Major-General Fry. The defensive perimeter within which this force was encamped extended over three and a half miles. During the flood season, from February to June, water varying in depth from one to four feet lies between Basrah and the further shore. There were two ways of crossing this sheet of water ; one by wading for about six miles and landing near Old Basrah, whence troops and convoys had to march another four miles before reaching Shaiba ; the other by using native boats called bellums. The latter approach crosses nearly eight miles of water and is traversed by a creek too deep to wade.

On the 10th a party of the enemy's horsemen was seen near Shaiba, but they soon dispersed before our cavalry. On the 11th the enemy's cavalry occupied Barjisiyah wood, and some 4000 of his infantry moved into Shwebda. General Fry then reported that a serious engagement was imminent, whereupon General Melliss, with the 30th Brigade, which had just arrived from Egypt, and a mountain battery, was ordered to move out the following morning. At 7.30 a.m. on 12th April General Fry reported that he was being attacked in force from the south, that he was confident of being able to hold his own, but that he was not able to prevent the enemy from occupying Old Basrah. General Melliss' brigade, which had started off with the intention of wading to Old Basrah, was held up by the enemy and had to return. He then tried to get there by bellum, but the Arab boatmen *en bloc* refused to assist. Sepoys, however, took their places, and at half-past eight that night General Melliss arrived at Shaiba, with most of the 24th Punjabis under Lieutenant-Colonel S. H. Climo,[1] and assumed command. The next day the enemy succeeded in cutting off Shaiba from Basrah, so that these were the only reinforcements that it was found possible to send.

Altogether on the 12th the enemy made four separate attacks, all of which were repulsed. At 3.30 a.m. the following morning another attack was made. Some small parties of the enemy succeeded in getting close up to our entanglements, and one of them, imitating German methods of warfare, called out *in Urdu,* " Do not fire ! "

The enemy were now surrounding the camp on all but the water side, and so on the 13th, early in the day, General Melliss decided to take the offensive. The 7th Lancers, under Lieutenant-Colonel Chesney Cook, made a gallant charge on a point known as North Mound. One squadron went for the mound itself ; the remaining squadrons made a gallant attempt to clear the enemy from the palm groves. Hand-to-hand fighting ensued,

[1] Now Major-General Sir Skipton Climo, K.C.B., D.S.O. He was wounded at Shaiba, and again at Ctesiphon.

and before the 7th Lancers retired they inflicted heavy losses on the enemy. Major Wheeler, who was killed, was awarded posthumously the Victoria Cross for his gallantry on this occasion. Our artillery now concentrated on the mound and adjacent buildings, and General Melliss pushed out from the perimeter, along which the whole force was now distributed, three battalions, taken from the north face, under the command of General Delamain. The infantry advanced towards the north-west, and with great dash captured North Mound, where two guns were secured. The cavalry brigade on the right flank succeeded in getting home into the now broken enemy and accounting for about 150 of them. Our attacking line, which was subsequently increased, continued to advance and by dint of hard fighting cleared the whole of the vicinity of the camp, driving back the enemy as far as South Mound and inflicting heavy losses on them. At this stage General Melliss thought it prudent to break off the action in order to rest his overwrought troops who had been under arms continuously throughout the previous night. On the morning of the 14th it was ascertained that the enemy had withdrawn to Barjisiyah wood, where they had established themselves very strongly. Considerable numbers of Mujahidin and Arab tribesmen, the very people in fact who had been urging the Turks to make this attack, withdrew from Barjisiyah during the night of the 13th. On the early morning of the 14th General Melliss, from his tower of observation on Kiln mound on the perimeter, noticed some of the enemy withdrawing from Barjisiyah wood towards Nakhailah. These eventually also proved to be Mujahidin and Arab tribesmen. In this indistinct

movement General Melliss saw an opportunity of
following up the blow which the enemy had been
dealt the day before, and he immediately decided
to resume the offensive without waiting for reinforcements.   He accordingly ordered the whole
force, less a camp garrison, to start off at 9 a.m. and
attack the enemy wherever found.   It soon became
evident that the enemy occupied a front of nearly
three and a half miles, but owing to mirage and to
our possessing no aircraft, it was quite impossible
to make any reconnaissance of the enemy's position.
So baffling was the mirage that at one time desperate
fighting was going on at decisive ranges without
either side being able to see the other.   The
enemy's trenches were well sited and practically
invisible from the front, while the smooth slope
of the ground towards Barjisiyah wood afforded
them an ideal position for defence.   By 1 p.m.
very heavy firing had become general all along the
line, but at 3 p.m. the fight was practically
stationary, the enemy clinging to his trenches
with desperate tenacity.   At last day began to
wane, and the battle being still undecided,   General
Melliss ordered a general advance.   The splendid
practice which our guns had been making throughout the day had already begun to tell.   The
Norfolks and the 120th Infantry, commanded
respectively by Colonel Peebles and Major Pocock,
under a terrific fire, dashed at the enemy's trenches
with the bayonet, whilst the 110th, also under a
heavy fire, pressed forward on the right supported
by "S" Battery under Lieutenant-Colonel C. A.
Sykes, and dismounted cavalry fire.   Almost
simultaneously the 16th Brigade, consisting of
the Dorsets, 24th Punjabis, 119th, and some of
the 117th, made a general advance, and about

5 p.m. the enemy's forward trenches fell into our hands, though not before the defenders had been killed almost to a man, the few survivors being taken prisoners. The day was won.

The return to camp, originally timed for 5.30 p.m., was not begun till 6 o'clock owing to the difficulty of collection and removal of wounded. Our withdrawal was entirely unmolested, and the troops reached Shaiba at 8.30 that night. Our casualties during this three days' battle amounted to 61 British officers killed and wounded, and over 1200 other ranks. The Dorset Regiment alone had 16 officers killed and wounded. The enemy's losses were estimated at 3000. I should like to quote the actual words of General Melliss, who is himself the possessor of a Victoria Cross :—

" It is impossible to conceive a more exposed tract of ground than the plain, devoid of cover, over which our infantry had to attack the Turkish trenches, cleverly concealed and sited. Our advance over the last four hundred yards was down a glacis-like slope. It was on the crest of this slope that so many of our losses occurred. Splendid dash combined with resolute courage alone carried our men across that bullet-swept glacis. It was a sheer dogged soldiers' fight, and no words of mine can express my admiration of the conduct of those gallant regiments who won through."

The regiments most heavily engaged during the night of the 12th–13th and throughout the 13th were General Delamain's troops, consisting of the Dorset Regiment, 24th Punjabis, 104th Rifles, and the 119th Infantry; and the Norfolk Regiment and 48th Pioneers under Lieutenant-Colonel Peebles. The severest fighting took place on the 14th, the brunt of which fell on the troops as follows :—

16th Brigade—General Delamain ; Dorset Regiment, 117th Mahrattas, 119th Infantry.

18th Brigade—General Fry ; Norfolk Regiment, 110th Mahrattas, 120th Rajputana Infantry.

30th Brigade—General Melliss ; 24th Punjabis (less one double company). General Melliss himself was in supreme command in the field.

Cavalry Brigade — General Kennedy ; 7th Lancers, 16th Cavalry, 33rd Cavalry ; " S " Battery, R.H.A.

Royal Artillery — Lieutenant-Colonel Cleeve, R.F.A. ; 63rd and 76th Batteries, R.F.A., 23rd Mountain Battery.

Royal Engineers—Lieutenant-Colonel Evans, R.E. ; 17th and 22nd Companies, 3rd Sappers and Miners.

During the night the enemy evacuated Barjisiyah and fled across the desert, scarcely halting till they reached Khamisiyah, a distance of nearly ninety miles from the scene of their defeat. They had got most of their guns away on the evening of the 14th, and the remainder were removed during the night. Throughout their retreat they were harassed and robbed by their former allies the Arabs. Thus ended another " smart little affair in the Gulf." One curious fact that became noticeable during this battle was that the enemy avoided surrendering to British regiments, and always gave themselves up where possible to the nearest Indian troops.

The Turks' right and left wings having now been crushed, it was decided to advance against their centre on the Tigris where they were reported to have six battalions and ten guns, with about 600 Mujahidin and double that number of armed tribesmen. The operation was entrusted to Major-

General Townshend, whose force consisted of the 16th and 17th Brigades, with the Norfolk Regiment, the 48th Pioneers, and one Field, one Mountain, one Howitzer, and two Heavy Batteries. The enemy's main position was at Bahran-Rotah-Maziblah-Sakricha, with advanced posts on Norfolk Hill, One Tree Hill, One Tower Hill, and Gun Hill. The whole country was under water. General Townshend's plan was to make a combined frontal and flank attack, the frontal to be the decisive one, and at the same time to make demonstrations to the west of the Tigris and up the Suwaib creek. The plan was completely successful, the chief features of the attack being a stirring bayonet charge by the Oxford and Bucks L.I., and the capture of One Tree Hill by the 22nd Punjabis. Early in the morning of 1st June our recently arrived aircraft discovered the enemy to be in full retreat, whereupon General Townshend left the 6th Division to concentrate at Bahran and pushed on up the river, past the sunken lighters at the mouth of the Rotah creek (another abortive attempt, like that above Muhammareh, to block the river) to Ezra's Tomb, which was reached at nightfall. On 2nd June a start was made at 2 o'clock in the morning, and by 4.20 a.m. the *Espiegle* was shelling the Turkish gunboat *Marmaris* which was soon holed in three places and set on fire. The river here began to shallow, and at a point about seven miles from Ezra's Tomb the sloops found they could get no further. Qal'at Salih was reached at 3.20 that afternoon, after some cavalry and a company of infantry had been dispersed with a few shells. White flags were now to be seen everywhere along the banks. At 1.30 p.m. on 3rd June, the King's Birthday, the town of 'Amarah

6

surrendered to General Townshend, who at the time
had actually with him only 22 men. Notwith-
standing this, 700 Turkish regular troops, including
the remnants of the two battalions of the Constantinople Fire Brigade, laid down their arms in
the barracks at 'Amarah, after which they were
put on board lighters to be sent down the river.
On 4th June the Norfolk Regiment arrived, and
none too soon, as by this time the Arabs had discovered how few men General Townshend had
with him and had started a fusillade in the town.
The surprising features of these operations were
the rapidity and bluff with which they were conducted. General Townshend had fought a very
successful action and had covered a distance of
about ninety miles, and all between the 31st May
and 1.30 p.m. on the 3rd of June.

On 18th June the 12th Brigade (less the 44th
Merwaras), under Lieutenant-Colonel H. H. Dunlop,
consisting of the Royal West Kent Regiment, the
67th and 90th Punjabis, and 82nd Battery, R.F.A.,
and the 7th Lancers, reached 'Amarah, having
marched across from the Karun River, *via* Bisaitin,
Umm Chir, Mazlag, and Halfiyah, through heat
that must have been well-nigh insupportable.

It was now decided to send a force up the
Euphrates with the object of occupying Nasiriyah,
a town of great strategical importance at the
junction of the Shatt-al-Hai and the Euphrates.
The Shatt-al-Hai, or Shatt-al-Gharaf as it is often
called, is a small river connecting the Tigris and
Euphrates, and from March to June is navigable
for large steamers. The advance began at the
end of June, when a force under Major-General
Gorringe left Kurna and moved up the unsurveyed
waters of the Euphrates. The Hakikah Channel,

through which that river enters the Hammar Lake, was found to have been blocked by a dam which the enemy had laboriously thrown across it.   This dam had to be demolished, and the opening of the channel caused the formation of a rapid up which the steamers and barges had to be hauled by parties of soldiers on the banks.   The rapids having been passed, the enemy were found in an advanced position near Suq-ash-Shuyukh.   After severe fighting they were dislodged, and on 5th July Suq-ash-Shuyukh surrendered.   From here · they retired to a very strong, entrenched position higher up the river and astride of it, with their flanks resting on marshes, and it was found necessary to bring up the 12th Brigade, and later on the 18th Brigade also.   The British force, while waiting for its reinforcements, took up a position north of Asani and close to the Turkish trenches, and were attacked every night, though without result or serious casualties.   On the 14th General Gorringe made an attack which failed owing to our troops being surrounded by Arabs just as they were on the point of capturing a strong work on the right of the Turkish position, after a most gallant attack through the marshes by the 24th Punjabis. It was then decided to postpone further operations until the arrival of the 18th Brigade, under Lieutenant-Colonel Frazer.   Finally, on 24th July, after a fierce artillery bombardment, the 12th Brigade, under Lieutenant-Colonel H. Dunlop, successfully assaulted the Turkish trenches on the left bank.   The 30th Brigade, under Major-General Melliss, then carried his advanced trenches on the other bank, having had to force the passage of a canal in order to do so.   Not only had this canal to be bridged, but the bridging materials had to be brought up in an armed barge which had to fight its way to the mouth of the canal. Though the Turks had suffered heavily from our artillery fire, they made a most determined resistance, and our men had to face a very heavy fire before they got in with the bayonet. Not without much hand-to-hand fighting was the whole position captured, but by noon this had been successfully accomplished. A second strong position had been prepared about two miles further on ; but by this time the enemy's resistance had been broken, and before sunset the bulk of them had retired northwards into the marshes with a loss of all their guns, five hundred killed, and several hundred prisoners.

In describing the great endurance displayed by this force, General Sir John Nixon says that they were fighting night and day with little intermission from the 5th to the 25th July. A shade temperature of 113° was often experienced, and that too in an atmosphere of the heaviest and closest humidity. The exhaustion and hardships of trench warfare, where guns, ammunition, and stores had to be moved without the help of animals, were in such circumstances difficult to describe. Twenty days of such work, culminating in an attack of a series of entrenched positions, formed a test of endurance which could scarcely be surpassed.

CHAPTER VI

EVENTS LEADING UP TO THE CAPTURE
OF BASRAH

THE following notes were jotted down from conversations with various Turkish officers in the Ministry of War, Constantinople, during the winter of 1918–19, and may contain certain points of interest.

When war was declared the Turkish forces in Mesopotamia consisted of the 12th and 13th Army Corps, which were composed entirely of local Arabs. These two corps were thought by the Ministry of War to be of little value, and were neglected in consequence. Whenever a Turkish officer spoke to the author about the " Irak divisions," meaning the 35th, 36th, 37th, and 38th, he always seemed to do so with an air of contempt which in reality they did not deserve. Attached to the 38th Division, however, was a battalion of which the officers and men were all Turks. This battalion, namely, the 1st/26th Regiment, which really formed part of the 9th Division of the 3rd Army Corps in Gallipoli, was sent out to Basrah during the summer of 1914 and belonged to one of the best regiments in the Turkish Army. Certainly no unit in any Irak division could compare with them. The composition of the 12th and 13th Army Corps was as follows :—

12th A.C.

35th Division (103rd, 104th, 105th Regiments).—At Mosul. From the Mesopotamian command it was transferred to the 18th Army Corps and then to the 13th Army Corps. The 104th and 105th Regiments were engaged at Barjisiyah in mid-April 1915. When disbanded a year later it belonged to the 6th Army.

36th Division (106th, 107th, 108th Regiments).—At Kerkuk. Was transferred with the headquarters of the 12th Army Corps to the Fourth Army in Syria. At the beginning of 1916 joined the Third Army and was engaged in the Caucasus operations. Disbanded 12th September 1916 and reformed as the 36th Caucasus Regiment. In the summer of 1918 reformed as the 36th Caucasus Division in the Ninth Army. Disbanded at the end of 1918, its units being distributed among other divisions.

13th A.C.

37th Division (109th, 110th, 111th Regiments).—At Baghdad. Almost destroyed whilst with the Sixth Army in Mesopotamia in 1915-16. Reformed in September 1916 as the 37th Caucasus Regiment and engaged in the fighting there. Afterwards became the 37th Caucasus Division. Sent to Constantinople in 1918, whence D.H.Q. went to Derinje and the three regiments to the Yildirim Army Group. When the 110th Regiment was destroyed there, the other two regiments were transferred to the 1st Division.

38th Division (112th, 113th, 114th, 1st/26th Regiments).—At Basrah. This division consisted of only six battalions of its own and one battalion attached, and suffered considerable casualties in the actions at Saniyah, Saihan, and Zain. Most of the remainder were captured at Kurna in December 1914, after which the division was disbanded, though remnants were still in existence at Barjisiyah.

Javid Pasha, who was Vali of Baghdad and Inspector of the 12th and 13th Army Corps at the outbreak of war, was relieved of his command in January 1915, and sent back to Constantinople as being inept and supine. He is not to be confused with the Javad Pasha, the capable and accomplished Turk who was Commander-in-Chief in the Dardanelles during the operations of the allied fleets in those straits, and who afterwards became Minister of War. The Vali of Basrah was Colonel Subhi Bey, who was taken prisoner at Kurna in December 1914.

It will be recalled that the first exchange of shots between the Turks and the British took place on the 6th November 1914. Fao was then a small Arab village, but it occupied a position of strategical value ; while the fact that it was the terminal station of the Turkish land telegraph line, which was connected with Persia and India by a British cable, invested it with a certain international importance. The capture of Fao was, in itself, a trifling affair and was achieved without a single casualty on our side. The Turkish losses only amounted to eight in all, but included the " Bimbashi of Fao Fort," a certain Captain Sidqi Bey, who was killed just as he and his little " Arab Frontier Company " were trying to make good their escape.

The force under Brigadier-General W. S. Delamain (now Lieutenant-General Sir Walter Delamain), which consisted of the 16th Infantry Brigade, then moved up the Shatt-al-'Arab and on 10th November disembarked on the right bank of the river a little way above Abadan. This camp became known as Saniyah from the fact of its being situated in a tract of *saniyah* land. During the first night ashore General Delamain got wind that the Turks were about to try and rush his camp, and at daybreak on 11th November the attempt was made. The actual assault was carried out by Turkish troops, namely the 1st Battalion of the 26th Regiment, but they were let down by the Arabs in support and the attack was easily repulsed. The Turkish commander, Sami Bey, who appears to have been regarded as a brave and talented young officer, was killed.

On 13th November Lieutenant-General (now Field-Marshal) Sir Arthur Barrett arrived at the mouth of the river and assumed supreme command. The Turkish headquarters were at a place called Baljaniyah, which is just above the town of Muhammareh, but of course on the opposite bank of the river.   A considerable force of the enemy, however, had established themselves at Saihan, four miles north-west of Saniyah, under the command of Major Adil Bey. This force, which consisted of the 2nd Battalion 112th Regiment, the 1st and 2nd Battalions of the 113th Regiment, a battalion of Basrah Gendarmerie, four field-guns, four mountain-guns, and four machine-guns, was attacked on 15th November by General Delamain and driven out with small loss to himself. On three or four separate occasions the writer referred to this action when talking to Major Adil Bey, but the latter always betrayed the same unwillingness to discuss the matter.   Nevertheless he admitted that the Turkish casualties amounted to 250 killed and wounded.

After the action at Saihan the enemy retired to Zain, where they were reinforced by a detachment of the 1st/26th and a troop of cavalry. Colonel Subhi Bey now took over the command in person. At daybreak on 17th November Sir Arthur Barrett moved out from Saniyah to attack the Zain position. The advance had to be made over flat ground without cover and rendered slippery by a heavy shower of rain during the forenoon, but it proceeded unchecked, and by sundown the position had been carried. Throughout this fight a house belonging to the Sheikh of Muhammarch was used by the Turks as general headquarters.

The 114th Regiment was not present at Zain, having been previously sent off by Subhi Bey to the small town of Abul Khasib. After his defeat at Zain, Subhi Bey retired with part of his force to Baljaniyah. Major Adil Bey, with the remainder, fell back on Abul Khasib, whence he retreated to Zubair, taking the 114th Regiment with him.

When discussing this action in Constantinople last January, a Turkish officer said to the writer :

" Kaimakam, you made a great mistake at Zain. Just as we were retiring and trying to get our guns away, *you stopped your guns from firing*. But for that our losses would have been doubled and we should have had to abandon all our guns. Why did your guns cease firing ? "

" Effendim," said I, " the English have a saying that God tempers the wind to the shorn lamb."

" Yes," said he, " of course we knew it was the will of God." In the midst of all these fine words

I could not bring myself to talk about dowdy economy ; so we left it at that.

His only other comments were that we were an honourable enemy, and that our bullets were very " merciful." The explanation of this latter remark is that our troops at Zain used the old conoidal bullet, which does not inflict so serious a wound as the pointed bullet, such as the 1st/26th Regiment used against us in the same action, or of course the leaden bullet used by the Irak regiments.

It has been decided that Sir Arthur Barrett's victory over the Turks on the 17th November 1914 is to be known officially as the " Affair of Sahil." It will be remembered that it was this engagement that delivered Basrah into the hands of the British. But it was more important as a political event than as a military exploit. The moral effect of it was far-reaching and out of all proportion to the number of troops engaged, because it determined the attitude of the inhabitants of vast regions. Moreover, it marked the establishment of the British in Mesopotamia.

It is interesting to note the curious way in which the official name arose. In some of our maps the word " Sahil " was printed across the particular riverain tract on the Shatt-al-'Arab in which the action was fought. The word means shore or beach, and is merely a topographical expletive such as marsh, arable land, cultivation, or any other. The proper name for the tract in question is Zain, and the old fort which was the objective of our right attack is called Kut-az-Zain. This engagement is always spoken of as Kut-az-Zain by the Turks, Germans, Arabs, and Persians. To call it Sahil because that word appeared on the map is unintelligent. A passenger arriving in Amiens by train might just as well pop his head out of the carriage-window and call the place Sortie, because he happened to see that word painted in large letters on the station wall.   To contend that a name, obviously in itself inaccurate, should be retained because it has become well known is to argue from false premises. On these unprogressive lines the villain of the Black Hole of Calcutta would still be known as Sir Roger Dowler.

Major Adil Bey informed the writer that the only maps of Mesopotamia they possessed were some they had found, at the outbreak of war, in the British vice-consulate at Mosul !

.

CHAPTER VII

THE ATTEMPT TO RECAPTURE BASRAH

THE Turkish attempt to recapture Basrah in mid-April 1915 resulted in three days' fighting which is known to the Turks as the battle of Barjisiyah and to us as that of Shaiba. The story of this battle from our point of view has been briefly told in a preceding chapter ; it is now proposed to give an account of it entirely from the Turkish side.

During the winter of 1918–19 the author found himself in Constantinople where, through the courtesy of the Turkish General Staff, he made the acquaintance of two Turkish officers who were present at Barjisiyah. One of these, Lieutenant-Colonel Ali Bey, of the Fire Brigade, was of great importance to our subject because, as will be seen, he was virtually in command throughout that battle. Moreover, he had kept a diary from the day he left Constantinople ; this diary, which he was good enough to hand over to me, was not intended for publication, or still less for perusal by a British officer, and is therefore of special value and interest. The other officer was Major Adil Bey, of the Turkish General Staff, who was in command of the Turkish force at the affair of Saihan on 15th November 1914, and was on the staff at the battle of Barjisiyah. The following account is compiled from the diary of Colonel Ali Bey, from cross-examinations to which both he and Major Adil Bey submitted with singular patience, and from the records in the Turkish Ministry of War.

The news of the defeat of Subhi Bey at Zain on 17th November 1914, and of the sudden collapse of the 38th Division, caused no little dismay at the Seraskerat in Stamboul, for they knew that the occupation of Basrah by Sir Arthur Barrett's division would follow in a few days. But however anxious the Turkish and German staff under Enver Pasha may have been that the British should be expelled from Irak, they were not going to be drawn into sending any considerable number of Turkish-speaking troops so far away from the capital as the Basrah vilayet. On 22nd November, that is to say the day before the Union Jack was hoisted in Basrah, Enver Pasha sent for Ali Bey and ordered him to form two new Fire-Extinguishing battalions from existing units and to mobilise them for service in Mesopotamia. This was done forthwith, and two splendid battalions, each consisting of 21 officers and 1030 men, with two machine-guns borrowed from the 5th Regiment, left Constantinople on 3rd and 4th December respectively.

Thus, within ten days of the fall of Basrah, the first batch of reinforcements for that front left the capital. Others were to follow. Ali Bey says :—
" The 2nd Battalion paraded on the square in front of the Ministry of War at 5 p.m. to-day (3rd December). Enver Pasha came out and said good-bye to the troops. Headed by the band, we then marched down to Sirkidje, where we took

boats and crossed over to Haidar Pasha. This battalion, which I accompanied, left Haidar Pasha at 11 p.m. for Bozanti."

Then follows a description of their journey. From Bozanti they marched to Tarsus, whence they went by rail to Alexandretta. From there they marched to Katma, where they again entrained. On 20th December they reached Jerablus, on the Euphrates, and four days later they set out on their long journey down the river. Their fleet consisted of no less than eighty *shakhturs* each capable of carrying thirty-two men. The officers' and machine-gun section's horses were loaded in the *shakhturs*, the remainder being sent by road to Feluja. They reached Nasiriyah on 27th January 1915, so that their journey from Constantinople had taken them fifty-four days. The following is an appreciation of the situation, and a summary of the events from 28th January, according to Ali Bey.

On arrival at Nasiriyah Ali Bey received long instructions from Lieutenant-Colonel Sulaiman Askeri, General Staff. Ali Bey was appointed to the command of the Right Wing and informed that henceforth he would be responsible for the organisation and preparation of the troops and tribesmen as far as operations were concerned, and also for the lines of communication. Up to 28th January the Right Wing command had consisted of the following remnants of the 38th Division :—

2 Arab battalions of about 400 men each.
1 squadron of cavalry.
1 field battery of 6 guns (not Q.F.).
2 mountain guns (not Q.F.).
1 field hospital section.

There were also the Arab tribesmen under " Saaduni Ajaimi Bey " and Abdullah Falih Bey. Also some of the Nejef tribes.

The Arab tribes of Mesopotamia are valueless. They were armed with the old pattern Mauser, with black powder ammunition. These arms and ammunition had been captured from the Turkish troops which had been sent from time to time to try and restore order amongst the Arabs. Most of the officers in the Irak divisions were Arabs having no authority with their men. The civil administration in these parts was very weak, so the Turks had to depend entirely upon Turkish troops.

After the fall of Basrah, Javid Pasha, the Vali of Baghdad, made overtures to Ajaimi in order to get the benefit of his personal influence. Ajaimi accepted mainly with a view to revenging himself on Saiyyid Talib and also to try and make good the losses to his property in the Muntafik country.

In addition to Ajaimi there were some *saiyyids*, such as Saiyyid Muhammad Habubi and Saiyyid Hadi, both from Kerbela ; and Sheikh Bakir, from Suq-ash-Shuyukh. These persons had thrown in their lot with the Turks on account of the proclamation of a *jihad*, but at the same time they were selling their rice to the British. This was the situation when Ali Bey took over the command of the Right Wing. One of the Arab battalions mentioned above, the field battery, the field hospital, as well as the Nejef tribes, were then at Nasiriyah. The other Arab battalion, the cavalry squadron, the two mountain guns, and Ajaimi's tribesmen were at Alawi. At that time some of the Kurdish tribes from the Sulaimaniyah and Kerkuk districts had sent down mounted contingents under the members of parliament for those places. These personages had telegraphed to Constantinople exaggerating the number of men they had sent, and saying that they had paid all their expenses up to Nasiriyah. In reality, the men were being paid by Sulaiman Askeri at the rate of two piastres a day for each infantryman, and two and a half piastres a day for each mounted man, besides forage for his horse.

The Osmanjik battalion, under Sulaiman Askeri, was being brought from the Kurna to the Right Wing command, together with the remainder of the 1st/26th Regiment, which had been sent to Basrah before the war, when Sulaiman Shefik Pasha was Vali of that city. The 1st/26th Regiment had taken part in all the fighting up to Basrah, and had lost so heavily that the battalion was now reduced to about a hundred and seventy men. Two howitzers were being sent to the Right Wing command, and the remnants of the 35th Division. All these units arrived in Nasiriyah between 28th January and 28th March. Communication was established between the Tigris and the Euphrates along the Shatt-al-Gharaf, and food depots were organised at Khamisiyah, Ghabisiyah, and Nakhailah. The Arab battalion from Nasiriyah, with a field battery and some tribesmen, were sent down to Nakhailah to put that place into a state of defence and to get into touch with the British. Those portions of the 35th Division which arrived first were sent on to Khamisiyah to support the advance troops at Nakhailah. The 35th Division consisted of two regiments of two battalions each, namely, the 104th and 105th Regiments, each battalion being about 600 strong ; an engineer company ; a cavalry squadron ; an artillery battalion of two batteries, each battery of six guns, not Q.F. ; a divisional military band ; and a field hospital. The 103rd Regiment, consisting of two battalions, each 600 strong, was sent to the Kurna command.

The 35th Division was formed after the Balkan War, and belonged to the Mosul Army Corps. It was composed of men from the Mosul area and had no fighting value. At the outbreak of the Great War the division was sent to Aleppo, but for some reason unknown to Ali Bey, it was recalled to Baghdad. When it arrived at Mosul a great many of the men deserted, and the result was that the ranks of the division were filled up with untrained and undisciplined Arabs from the Mosul area who were only soldiers in dress. The Osmanjik battalion, and what was left of the 1st/- 26th Regiment, arrived at Nasiriyah about the middle of March. The advance was then about to take place. The commander of the whole force, Sulaiman Askeri, arrived about the same time. He had been severely wounded and was being carried about on a stretcher.

Sulaiman Askeri Bey had passed through the Ecole Militaire, Constantinople, and was therefore a trained Staff Officer. His early military life was spent in the Monastir district hunting down Bulgarian brigands. After the Constitution he went to Baghdad when Nazim Pasha was Vali there, and thus he became acquainted with Mesopotamia. In the Italian War in Tripoli in 1911 he went to Benghazi, where he remained, in the dress of an Arab, for a year under Enver. In the Balkan War his personality and fearlessness earned for him a great name. It is a remarkable man who, amongst brave men, distinguishes him-

7

self by his bravery.   During the advance of the
Turkish Army from Bulair to Adrianople he crossed
the frontier and entered Bulgaria.   At the end of
that war he resigned, but his resignation was not
accepted.   At the outbreak of the Great War
it was considered desirable by the Committee of
Union and Progress to send him as far away from
Constantinople as possible, so with 450 selected
men he left that city for Baghdad.

Before the arrival of the Fire Brigade he had
attacked the British at Kurna, where he was
wounded.   One bullet hit him in the left leg
below the knee, breaking the bone, and another hit
him in the hip.   As his cure would take perhaps
six months, he became depressed and returned to
Baghdad.   The Ministry of War sent out Lieutenant-
Colonel Kiazim Bey to take his place, but on the
arrival of that officer in Baghdad Sulaiman Askeri
telegraphed to Constantinople that he would not
hand over his command ; so Kiazim Bey returned.
Wounded and weak, Sulaiman Askeri travelled
from Baghdad down to Shatrah by boat, and on to
Nasiriyah in a stretcher.   On his arrival there all
the sheikhs and saiyyids came troubling him
" about money and nonsense."   There was little
talk of duty and preparation for fighting.

On 27th March the 35th Division was pushed
forward to Khamisiyah, and the Nasiriyah force
crossed over to the south bank of the Euphrates
at Shamiyah.   The troops of the Right Wing
command, and the tribesmen, were to attack
Shaiba on 12th April.   This order was issued
to the Right and Left Wings and also to the Kurna
command.

The information available regarding the British
force was as follows.   The advanced Turkish

troops at Nakhailah had come into contact with the British. But Saifullah Bey, who was in command there, and Ajaimi, had been sending in fanciful reports of no military value, and so, when the 35th Division arrived in Khamisiyah, the officer commanding the division took over charge of the Nakhailah post. On 3rd, 8th, and 16th March he made reconnaissances and reported that the following units had been identified as being present with the British force at Shaiba :—

> 103rd Light Infantry.
> 120th Infantry.
> 2nd Battalion Norfolk Regiment.
> 7th Rajputs.
> 33rd Cavalry.
> 76th Battery, R.F.A.
> 30th Mountain Battery.
> 48th Pioneers.
> 17th Signal Company.

It was known that the Shaiba towers (*qasr*) were fortified, and also that it was possible to reinforce any part of the British line with troops from Basrah.

The order of battle of the Right Wing command, and the tribesmen, concentrated between Shamiyah and Nakhailah was, on 27th March 1915, as follows :—

REGULARS.

Headquarters of the Right Wing Command.

> 15 officers.
> 92 other ranks.

Headquarters of the 35th Division.
14 officers.
101 other ranks.

104th Regiment.
44 officers.
1450 other ranks.

105th Regiment.
41 officers.
1395 other ranks.

Cavalry Squadron of the 35th Division.
2 officers.
70 other ranks.

Artillery Battalion.
19 officers.
335 other ranks.
12 field guns.
533 rounds common shell.
2135 rounds shrapnel shell.

Engineering Company.
2 officers.
80 other ranks.

Cavalry Squadron.
3 officers.
95 other ranks.

1st Muretteb Battalion.
(The Osmanjik Battalion and the 1st/26th
Regiment.)
17 officers.
729 other ranks.

The Fire-Extinguishing Regiment.

43 officers (including Ali Bey).
2046 other ranks.

Muretteb Irak Regiment.
(2 Arab battalions.)

39 officers.
850 other ranks.

Muretteb Field Battery.

4 officers.
216 other ranks.
5 field guns (not Q.F.).
412 rounds common shell.
600 rounds shrapnel shell.

Mountain Artillery Section.

1 officer.
50 other ranks.
3 mountain guns.[1]
333 rounds common shell.
74 rounds shrapnel shell.

Howitzer Section.

1 officer.
58 other ranks.
2 howitzers (10·5 cm.).
500 rounds common shell.
200 rounds shrapnel shell.

---

[1] Probably a mistake for two.

Cavalry Squadron.

2 officers.
80 other ranks.
The above numbers *include* non-combatants.
Total : 247 officers and 7647 other ranks, with 22 guns.

TRIBESMEN.

With Ajaimi Bey.

6153 foot.
630 horse.

With Abdullah Falih Bey.

1550 foot.
1000 horse.

Mujahidin of Shamiyah and Hindiyah.

1027 foot.
211 horse.

El Bedur, El Khafajah, Abu Sa'id, and El Husainat Tribes.

930 foot.
600 horse.

Kurdish Mujahidin.

175 foot.
1134 horse.

Janun-el-Ubaiyid.

800 foot.
81 horse.

With Saiyyid Hadi.
4032 foot.
36 horse.

Totals : 14,667 foot.
3,692 horse.
——— Tribesmen, 18,359
Regulars, 7,894

Grand total, 26,253 [1]

The numbers of these tribesmen changed every day. It was to the advantage of the sheikhs to exaggerate the strength of their following because they were being paid so much per man. Their rifles were of many kinds, much worn, very dirty, and mostly without backsights. The tribesmen had no modern fighting value, and, moreover, no love for the Turks. On 30th March most of the Jaf, Hamawend, and Nejef tribes deserted from Nakhailah and went back to Khamisiyah. Sulaiman Askeri said that in the Turkish Army there was no place for deserters, and sent them to their homes. This shows the futility of trusting to these tribesmen. The Nakhailah Arabs said that the British position at Shaiba was an open one and could be stormed in an hour. At the same time they were writing to Sulaiman Askeri that if the attack were really going to take place they would not remain. They were telling the British that the Turks would not attack, and they were

[1] This was on 27th March. Many desertions took place between that date and 12th April, when Sulaiman Askeri's total force at Barjisiyah, including non-combatants, probably did not exceed 18,000 men.

telling the Turks that the British had evacuated
Shaiba.   The result of all this was that the
Turks knew that their attack on Shaiba would
fail, but as Sulaiman had given his word to Enver
Pasha, the attack would have to take place.

The organisation of the lines of communication
on 27th March was as follows :—Along the
Euphrates line, provisions and stores came to
Nasiriyah by river.   From the Tigris line they
came by the Shatt-al-Gharaf as far as Shatrah by
steamer, from Shatrah to Decheh by small boat,
and then on to Nasiriyah by land.   From Nasiriyah   to   Khamisiyah,   Suq-ash-Shuyukh,   and
Suwaichah,   by   *mahailah*   and   *bellem*.   From
Suq-ash-Shuyukh and Suwaichah to Ghabisiyah
via Sinafur by river.   The British motor boats at
the last-named place did no harm at all.   Two
Turkish steamers and two motor boats assisted in
the transport work.   From Ghabisiyah the troops
used their own transport for carrying their rations.
In Nasiriyah there were large supply and munition
dumps.   When the British took to shelling the
transport by means of guns put on to *mahailahs*,
the Turks had to withdraw their depot on the
water's edge at Ghabisiyah to a point inland, and
they sent two guns and a company of infantry to
guard it.

·On the morning of 28th March, at five o'clock,
the Fire Brigade, which was on the Shamiyah side
of the river, the 1st Muretteb Battalion, a field
battery under the command of a German reserve
officer, the howitzer section, the Kurdish volunteers,
and the headquarters of the Right Wing command
started for Abu Salibiq.   The track had been put
in order beforehand, and the march was an easy
one.   The following morning they again made

an early start and got as far as Khamisiyah. Immediately on arrival there the 35th Division and the ammunition columns were sent on to Ghabisiyah, and on the afternoon of 2nd April the remainder of the troops in Khamisiyah went forward. The first halt was made at Hamadah, the second at Legait, and the third at Ghabisiyah. By 4th April all the troops had reached Ghabisiyah, whence some were sent on to Nakhailah. The Right Wing troops, after spending a night at Rumailah, reached Nakhailah on 8th April. Ten days' rations for the troops had been sent here on camels. The advanced troops already in Nakhailah now rejoined their units.

The Staff Officer, who had been sent on ahead to make reconnaissances and to study the ground over which the attack was to be made, now reported as follows :—" The enemy have made no fortifications at Barjisiyah, Zubair, or round about there. The ground is gently undulating. There are no British troops or fortifications on the Shaiba mounds lying north and south-east of the Barjisiyah-Kuwaibdah [1] line. From these mounds Shaiba itself is distant about four kilometres. On this rising ground there are a few shallow trenches knee-deep. The enemy have entrenched themselves strongly on the south-east of the line of the Shaiba towers. Behind this position, on the *khor* side, many tents are to be seen. The British advanced line is about 500 metres in front of the Shaiba towers. About half an hour before sunset the Turkish reconnoitring troops went to the northern entrance to Zubair, and at sunset they approached to within a couple of kilometres of Shaiba. Both sides opened fire, the

[1] Shwebda on our maps.

enemy being reinforced by an infantry company and two machine-guns. They also sent some cavalry and a battery towards their left flank. From this skirmish we got the impression that the British force and position were of considerable strength.

The question of water was one of great importance to the attack. There were only two watering places, Barjisiyah and Zubair, of which the former was much the better. The Turks were therefore obliged to make a dangerous flank march close to the enemy's position round the Shaiba towers. A squadron of regular cavalry and some mounted tribesmen now made a reconnaissance round about Barjisiyah, Zubair, and Kuwaibdah.

On the night of 10th April the force moved towards Barjisiyah in two columns, and on the 11th reached the wood before sunrise. After digging trenches the tired troops were given a rest. There were no signs that the enemy had discovered them. The men were forbidden to leave the wood or to light fires. At 3 p.m. Ali Bey, with the commanding officers, made a reconnaissance, moving at first towards Zubair and then towards Shaiba. The enemy opened fire on them with all three arms, but they gained a useful knowledge of the ground. When they got back to Barjisiyah Wood, Sulaiman Askeri Bey, who was lying on a stretcher, gave orders to attack, which were as follows :—

" OPERATION ORDERS, RIGHT WING COMMAND.
" Barjisiyah Wood, 11*th April* 1915.

" 1. To-day the enemy opened artillery and machine-gun fire on our cavalry patrols on a line south-west from Markab Shaiba towers.

" 2. The troops of the Right Wing command

will attack the enemy's position to-morrow morning before sunrise. The troops and *mujahidin* will creep up close under cover of the darkness. The objective of the attack is the Shaiba *qasr*.

" 3. Ajaimi Bey and his tribesmen will attack at right angles to the line of the Markab Shaiba towers ; the 1st Muretteb Battalion to the left of this line ; the Fire Brigade to the right of this line, advancing from a north-westerly direction. The 104th Regiment, from the centre of the north-western exit of Barjisiyah Wood, facing north, will attack the south mounds of Shaiba. The Muretteb Irak Regiments, with two mountain guns and the *mujahidin* of Abdullah Falih Bey, under Major Vedad Bey, will attack in the same direction. The Hindiyah and Shamiyah *mujahidin*, under Saiyyid Muhammad Habubi and Captain Shevket Bey, will attack the Shaiba mounds between the *khor* and the troops under Vedad Bey. The 105th Regiment, the cavalry squadron, and the Kurdish horsemen under Deputy Zia Bey, will be in reserve at the exit of Barjisiyah Wood which faces Shaiba. Ajaimi Bey will send some of his men in the direction of Gurmat Ali. The mounted men of Abdullah Falih Bey will attack the enemy's right flank. The Muretteb field battery will take up a position in rear of the centre of the Fire Brigade on a spot which has been pointed out to-day to the artillery commander. The artillery battalion of the 35th Division will take up a position, which will be pointed out, in rear of the 104th Regiment. The howitzers will take up a position in rear of the Fire Brigade Regiment.

" 4. Artillery and infantry units will replenish their ammunition under their own arrangements.

" 5. A field hospital will be established behind the Fire Brigade and the 1st Muretteb Battalion. A second field hospital will be established in rear of and between the 104th Regiment and the Muretteb Irak Regiment. Some field hospital sections will be located at the exit of Barjisiyah Wood.

" 6. My position will be in rear of and between the Fire Brigade and the 104th Regiment.

" 7. The Engineer Company will prepare the artillery emplacements and will destroy obstacles.

" (Signed)   ALI BEY, Lieut.-Colonel,
" O.C. Right Wing."

The above operation orders were issued to Commanding Officers and to the Arab sheikhs, and were explained personally to the latter. Afterwards the orders were explained to everyone in the neighbourhood. The troops, who had been told to get as much sleep as possible before the attack, were roused at 10 p.m. and ordered to be ready to advance in two hours. By midnight the troops were formed up outside the wood ready to advance, and the tribesmen were concentrated at the eastern edge of the wood. The columns having been provided with experienced guides, the advance began. It was important, but at the same time not at all easy, for each unit to occupy the position allotted to it in the operation orders. Each regiment had its own scouts, and there were connecting files between the regulars and the tribesmen. The guns followed the infantry. The night was very dark. In this formation they marched on through the darkness without noise. In Shaiba some lights were seen,[1] which showed that the troops

[1] In spite of the strict orders of the G.O.C. at Shaiba.

were on the right line of march. The sun was now
rising, and the infantry began to deploy. They
approached the enemy's wire entanglements and
opened fire. The enemy withdrew his outposts
into the fort. It was now daylight, and the troops
took up their positions as ordered. The scouts
got to within 300 metres of the enemy's wire. At
first no movement of the enemy was observed in
the fort. Then they opened artillery, machine-
gun, and rifle fire, and their artillery fire increased.
We were unable to locate the enemy's batteries,
and so could not counter them. The enemy
silenced one of the Turkish batteries, but the others
remained in action, though apparently without
much effect. The slow rate of fire and the erratic
shooting of the howitzers were due to the fact that
whilst the howitzers were Bulgarian, the ammunition for them was Serbian. The Turks realised
that they were attacking an entrenched position
which would be difficult to take. Their infantry,
being held up, entrenched themselves and opened
fire on the loopholes of Shaiba Fort, but without effect. Ajaimi Bey's troops, which had been
ordered to support the right flank of the Turkish
troops, were of no use at all, and towards noon
went off to drink water. The Irak Regiment, the
tribesmen, and the *saiyyids*, who were in Imam
Ans, attempted to advance, but were not able to
effect anything. The result was a lull in the fighting on the Turks' part. Their regular infantry
and artillery were not able to produce any moral
effect on the enemy or to induce the Arabs to
stand the enemy's artillery fire. The engineer
company were without sufficient means to cut
wire and destroy obstacles. It was hoped, under
cover of darkness, to destroy the enemy's wire

and to storm his trenches, but if this were not successful the Turks intended to retire to Barjisiyah before it got light, entrench themselves there, and await the enemy's counter-attack, thus forcing him to come out into the open.

The situation remained unchanged, and so Ali Bey went off to inform Sulaiman Askeri, who was watching the fight through field-glasses from an observation post at the eastern end of Barjisiyah Wood. They decided to make a general night attack, so Ali Bey returned and gave orders accordingly.

At dusk rifle fire started. The enemy replied with machine-gun and rifle fire, and sought out the Turkish columns with a searchlight which, however, was soon put out of action. The troops advanced to the barbed wire and tried to cut it. Time was passing. They were making no headway, and to have continued this attack would have been madness. The troops had not slept the night before and had been under heavy fire all day. At midnight Sulaiman Askeri's aide-de-camp came to Ali Bey to inquire how things were going. It was now reported that the enemy had been reinforced. Sulaiman Askeri insisted on renewing the attack at dawn, so Ali Bey issued the necessary orders.

The next attack started before sunrise. Still no progress was made. About noon Ali Bey gave the order to retire, but this order did not reach the 1st Battalion of the Fire Brigade, and they remained in their advanced position. At this juncture the enemy made a sortie with some infantry and cavalry towards Imam Ans and inflicted heavy losses on the Muretteb Irak Regiment. Again Ali Bey went to Sulaiman Askeri

and explained the situation to him. Sulaiman
Askeri sent a squadron of cavalry and a platoon
to Zubair to cover the retirement. He recommended sending one or two infantry battalions to
Zubair to try and envelop Shaiba from a
distance. Ali Bey opposed the plan, saying that
the Turkish losses had been very heavy, and that
the troops, and above all the tribesmen, were completely demoralised. Moreover, a counter-attack
was to be expected. The occupation of Zubair
would be of no use, as the inhabitants of that place
were only waiting to see which side won. All
Ajaimi's troops had run away except about thirty
who remained with him. Ali Bey knew that
after the first Turkish attack had failed Ajaimi had
gone into Zubair to see Sheikh Ibrahim and to
make some arrangement with him.

Sulaiman agreed that it would be no use to
occupy Zubair and ordered the troops to be withdrawn to Barjisiyah Wood during the night. The
104th Regiment, which had been in reserve, and
a squadron of cavalry were told off as rearguard.
About 400 severely wounded were to be sent back
to Nakhailah. The troops took up their positions
on the eastern side of the wood ready for a possible
attack in the morning. The night passed without
any fighting. About 8 a.m. reports were received
that enemy columns were on the move.

The dispositions were as follows :—The 1st
Muretteb Battalion was on the right flank, the
Fire Brigade in the centre, and the 104th Regiment
on the left. The remnants of the Irak Regiment
were towards Kuwaibdah. The 105th Regiment,
the Kurdish horsemen, and the Engineer company
were in Barjisiyah Wood in reserve. The battle
started, but up to noon the British infantry could

make no progress. The enemy made an attack on the left flank with his cavalry, but it was easily driven off, so the battle was now going well.   By 2 p.m. the Turkish troops in the firing-line, and especially the Fire Brigade, began to run out of ammunition, and it was not possible to get any up to them.   The non-combatants who were being used as ammunition carriers were mostly wounded. The weather was hot and water was scarce.   Many of the wounded returning from the firing-line had been hit in the right arm, hand, or foot.

The situation became critical.   The Turks were sure the enemy would not remain where they were, but with the night would return to Shaiba. Soon their shells began to fall short, and it was known that they had gone back.   At this moment part of the 1st Muretteb Battalion gave way, so some cavalry were sent to force them back into the firing-line.   A report was received from the Fire Brigade that their casualties had been very heavy, and that both their machine-guns had been put out of action.   The open character of the ground made it difficult to manœuvre.   The 104th Regiment, which had been not been engaged at all, began to retire.

In the evening the Turks fell back again, so Ali Bey went to Sulaiman Askeri and advised him to get away and to give orders for a general retirement. Very reluctantly, and with great disappointment, he agreed.   Ali Bey had not gone more than a couple of hundred yards from him when he heard a revolver shot.   Sulaiman Askeri had shot himself on his stretcher.

In the three days' fighting he had seen that the Arab tribesmen of Ajaimi and the Kurds, on whom he had placed such reliance, were of no use at all, and that for the failure of this attack he would be blamed by Enver.   So he committed suicide.

During the night orders were given for a retirement to Nakhailah as rapidly as possible, and it was carried out without molestation from the enemy.   Thus the attempt to recapture Basrah had failed, with great loss of life to the Turks and with the greater loss of Sulaiman Askeri.   During that night the Arabs fled in all directions, some across the *khor* in *bellems*, others across the desert on horseback.   Only Ajaimi and a few of his mounted men remained, like vultures to pick up what they could. At daylight the Turks sent two squadrons back towards Barjisiyah.   They reported that there was no enemy to the west of the wood.   Ajaimi insisted that the enemy would attack Nakhailah at once, but Ali Bey was not to be taken in by this ruse to induce him to abandon all his stores and ammunition.

On 15th April the Turks buried Sulaiman Askeri at Nakhailah, and then left again at 2 p.m. Some cavalry remained as rearguard.   Ali Bey with his force reached Ghabisiyah in tolerable order considering everything, and then left again at once for Khamisiyah, where they halted for four days.

At Khamisiyah Enver Pasha, from the Ministry of War in Constantinople, summoned Ali Bey to the telegraph office and asked for a report.   Ali Bey explained that, owing to the superiority of the enemy and the worthlessness of the tribesmen, the Turks had been driven back ; that the enemy had lost so heavily that there was no chance of the Turks being pursued or of Mesopotamia being further invaded for some time to come ; and that Ali Bey was trying to reorganise his forces.   After this Colonel Nureddin Bey was appointed to the

8

chief command of the forces in Mesopotamia.   At Khamisiyah Ali Bey formed a battalion from the remnants of the Irak Regiment, which he left there with two guns, and then went on to Nasiriyah with the rest of the force.   On arrival there it was reported that the enemy were bombarding the Haqiqah Dam, and all the inhabitants were getting ready to leave the town.   Ali Bey, however, stopped this and made arrangements for holding Nasiriyah with the remnants of the 35th Division.

Ali Bey then handed over the town to the Muntifik Area Command and went to Kut-al-Amarah with what remained of the Fire Brigade and the 1st Muretteb Battalion.   Colonel Nureddin Bey arrived in Baghdad from Constantinople in forty-two days, during which time nothing had happened. Ali Bey then went to Baghdad, handed over to Nureddin Bey, and left for the Caucasus front.

The casualties amongst the regular troops at Barjisiyah amounted to 54 officers and 2381 other ranks.   These figures do not include the very slightly wounded.   The casualties amongst the Arab and Kurdish tribesmen are unknown, but probably did not exceed a few hundred.   The bulk of the casualties occurred amongst the Turkish troops, namely, the Fire Brigade and the 1st Muretteb Battalion.   The Fire Brigade lost half its total strength.   Only five Arab officers were killed and wounded, which shows the part they had played in the fighting.   The majority of the Arabs who were missing rejoined the retreating tribes.   The diary concludes with the following remark :—" Although the Turks were so badly equipped and cared for, still we all felt proud because we had done our duty."

Vraiment, le courage—c'est une élégance.

Up to this point Turkish opinion only has been quoted. For the statements which follow there is merely the authority of the author.

After exhaustive inquiry the writer puts down the number of regular combatant troops at Barjisiyah at 240 officers and 6300 other ranks. Of these only the Fire Brigade and the 1st Muretteb Battalion were composed of real Turks. The total fighting strength of these two units on the night before the battle was 2550 of all ranks. It will therefore be urged by the military student who examines the order of battle given above that if Enver Pasha had really meant to recapture Basrah he would have sent more regular troops to that front. It must, however, be remembered that when the Fire Brigade left Constantinople the mobilisation of the Turkish Army had not long begun. Mighty events were happening everywhere almost daily, and for the time being the attention of the Ministry of War was absorbed in the forthcoming operations in the Caucasus. Furthermore, although Enver Pasha was himself anti-British, it was Russia, and not England, whom the Turkish nation regarded as its real enemy.

The Third Turkish Army crossed the Russian frontier on Christmas Eve, 1914. Two days later began a series of desperate encounters, known collectively as the Battle of Sari Kamish, which continued until 5th January. The frightful nature of this fighting, which is perhaps not generally realised, may be judged from the few following facts. At the time of crossing the frontier the 9th Army Corps comprised at least 18,000 combatants. At the end of December the whole corps could only muster a thousand men. The 10th Corps arrived in the Sari Kamish area on

29th December. Within two days its strength was reduced to a total of 2300 men. The 11th Corps suffered so severely that on 6th January it was found impossible to form one division out of its former three.

It was, therefore, only natural that for some time after this the eyes of the Turkish Empire should remain turned towards the blizzard that was sweeping down from the Caucasus, and that the Mesopotamian force should be lost sight of. Then came the British bombardments of the Dardanelles, warning the Turks that an army would be required in the Gallipoli Peninsula, and so it was reluctantly decided that no more troops could be spared for a front so far away from Constantinople as lower Mesopotamia. Still Enver Pasha never doubted that Sulaiman Askeri, with his 6300 regulars and his hordes of Arabs and Kurds, would retake Basrah.

It is interesting to note the extent to which the Shatt-al-Gharaf was used by the Turks for the Nasiriyah concentration, the Osmanjik Battalion, the 1st/26th Regiment, the 104th and 105th Regiments, and the field and mountain artillery all coming by this route.

According to Major Adil Bey there were altogether twenty-eight guns with the Turkish forces at Nasiriyah, which agrees with Sir Arthur Barrett's estimate. Ali Bey, however, stated definitely that only twenty-one guns—certainly not more than twenty-two—ever reached Barjisiyah.

It will be observed that when the orders for the attack had been issued to the Right and Left Wings and to the Kurna command, they were then "explained to everyone in the neighbourhood." This is, perhaps, the most significant sentence in

Ali Bey's diary. The Turks knew well that if they could defeat the British the whole countryside would rise and drive the invading infidel into the sea. Indeed, they encouraged the idea by holding out prospects of loot and by pointing to the merit of joining in a *jihad* which had been proclaimed by the Sultan of Turkey. Arabs from far and wide, as well as the whole Muslim population of Basrah, were only waiting to see who was going to win, when they would swoop down on the vanquished. Swarms of Arabs, who were domiciled in Persian territory, actually crossed the Shatt-al-Arab, so as to be on the spot when the time came. When they heard the Turks were retreating they all disappeared.

CONSTANTINOPLE,
January 1919.

CHAPTER VIII

GALLIPOLI IN 1914

WHEN the Austrian Crown Prince was murdered on the 28th June 1914, there were two German ships, *Goeben* and *Breslau*, cruising about in the Mediterranean. It soon became clear that this murder was to be made the occasion of a great war, and within a month of its occurrence the British Admiralty, with a foreknowledge of the war upon which they justly pride themselves, suspended the demobilisation of the fleet. But what of the *Goeben* and *Breslau?*

Before proceeding to deal with this subject it will be appropriate to make one or two preliminary observations.

In the first place, it should be realised that there are only two exits from the Mediterranean to the high seas, namely the Straits of Gibraltar and the Suez Canal, both of which are in the hands of the British. Therefore if these two German ships wanted to get out of the Mediterranean their only chance was to do so before war broke out. But of course it was not their intention to get out. Their objective was Constantinople, and they could not have been sent to the Mediterranean for any other purpose. Then it will be recalled that on the 4th August, the day on which Great Britain declared war on Germany, these two ships were calmly taking in supplies at Messina, and that immediately they received the news that England had come into the war they made a dash for the Dardanelles where they arrived on the 10th August.

For some years before the Great War it was pretty generally known that there was an alliance between Germany and Turkey, and that if war broke out and England joined in the first business of Germany would be to drag in Turkey. One would have thought, therefore, that almost before the ink on the Austrian ultimatum to Serbia was dry, British ships would have been rushed to the mouth of the Dardanelles with orders to cruise about near the edge of Turkish territorial waters and prevent any German ships from entering the straits. Yet the allied fleets in the Mediterranean were disposed in such a manner as to leave the road to Constantinople open. Nor was this all, for shortly afterwards a German merchantman laden with mines was smuggled up to Chanak. On August 15th a double line of contact mines was laid from Kephez to Suandere. More mines were laid on the 19th, and several Hotchkiss guns were mounted on both sides of the straits to guard the minefield. On the 24th the channel on the European side of the straits was further mined. The dates of these incidents are particularly interesting. The next event was the closing of the Dardanelles, on 27th September, by order of a German military officer. Nets and more mines were then put down, and numbers of German naval gunners were sent to man the Dardanelles forts. All this was done while Turkey was still a neutral power. Surely there is no more amazing episode in history.

If anyone at the outbreak of the Great War had

hazarded to describe the Gallipoli Peninsula as the key of the whole enemy position he would undoubtedly have been told that he had got the wrong end of the telescope to his eye. Many people would have been surprised at such a declaration, but the surprising part of it is that the pre-eminent importance of this peninsula came to be overlooked until it was too late.

As the Germans had command of the Black Sea, they decided that the most popular way for Turkey to enter the arena would be for that power to declare war on Russia. Accordingly two or three Turkish torpedo-boats raided Odessa on 29th October and sank the Russian gunboat *Donetz*. The French ship *Portugal* was damaged, two of her crew being killed and two wounded, and the Russian steamers *Vitiaz*, *Liazaref*, and *Whanpao*, damaged. Some loss of life was caused in the town itself by shell-fire.

Turkey was now at war. On 3rd November the outer forts of the Dardanelles were bombarded for about ten minutes by the British. The alleged object of this bombardment was to find out by a practical test the effective range of the guns of the Turkish forts. This unfortunate operation, which of course only served to put the Turks on the alert, was undertaken without any reference to the War Council or the War Office. The orders for it emanated solely from the Admiralty.

On 25th November the subject of an attack on the Dardanelles was mentioned at a meeting of the War Council, but Lord Kitchener considered that the moment for such an enterprise had not yet arrived, and the project was shelved. Thus matters stood until 2nd January 1915, when a very important telegram, which materially affected the situation, was received from our ambassador at Petrograd. A great battle was then raging in the Caucasus at Sari Kamish, and this telegram represented that, as the Russians were being somewhat hardly pressed, they wanted us to demonstrate against the Turks in some other quarter. The attack on the Dardanelles was thus more or less forced upon us, and had not been seriously considered up to the receipt of this telegram.

The possibilities of such an attack had first come under review in 1906. In December of that year the General Staff issued a memorandum on the subject, in which they stated that, in their opinion, unaided action by the fleet was to be deprecated ; that if combined operations were undertaken no landing could be effected on the Gallipoli Peninsula unless the co-operating naval squadron could guarantee with its guns that the landing force should reach the shore unmolested and find after disembarkation a sufficiently extended area, free from hostile fire, to enable them to form up for battle on suitable ground. In summing up, the General Staff stated that they did not consider that the co-operating fleet would be able to give this guarantee, and they recommended that such an operation should not be attempted.

The Admiralty, however, considered that this memorandum underrated the value of the assistance which the fleet could give, especially in the Gallipoli Peninsula where the hydrographical conditions are such that any number of vessels of the largest size and power could be employed to support the land forces ; that Turkey was less formidable in 1914 as a military power than was generally assumed ; that there had been a considerable improvement in naval ordnance since this memo-

randum was written in 1906 ; that the fall of the
Liège and Namur forts led to the conclusion that
permanent works could easily be dealt with by
modern long-range guns ; and that by the use of
aircraft the value of naval bombardment, especially
by indirect laying, would be enormously increased.

The case under review, however, is governed by
the principle that it is easier for a stationary
battery to hit an object moving at a given rate
than for a battery moving at that given rate to
hit a stationary object.   The truth of this statement had often been demonstrated empirically
and is well known.   Other things being equal,
floating batteries could never engage land batteries
with any chance of success, and the Dardanelles
bombardments proved conclusively that they cannot
do so even with an enormous superiority in power
and range on their side.   The experiment is not
likely to be tried again.   The Belgian forts were
not reduced by fire from floating batteries.   In the
Dardanelles, according to the testimony of the
American Ambassador, not a single gun had been
put out of action in any of the batteries visited by
him in March 1915.

The assistance which a fleet can give to a landing force is actually slight.   The ships, being unable
to remain within effective range of the land guns,
have to stand so far out that it is difficult to say
whether the moral effect is felt more by the defenders or by the attackers.   The belief now most generally held is that even if the allied navies had made
their attempt in November 1914, they would not
have succeeded single-handed, and that by post-
poning it until the following February they made
failure a certainty.

The essential preliminary to the forcing of the

Dardanelles was the occupation of the Gallipoli Peninsula from which the forts on both sides of the straits can be completely dominated, and those on the peninsula itself can be taken in reverse. In other words, under normal circumstances it would be a military operation carried out with the assistance of a fleet. But in the winter of 1914 the circumstances were not normal ; there were no soldiers to spare. The War Council decided that the main theatre of operations for the British military forces was France, and should remain so as long as French territory was liable to successful invasion and the French people required armed support.

At the inception of the scheme, the attack on the Dardanelles was intended to be a purely naval one, without involving the army at all. The Admiralty were optimistic over being able to force the straits by themselves, and the navy at large regarded the scheme as an attractive departure from their normal rôle of guarding the lines of communication. But the original idea of a purely naval attack was gradually abandoned, and the War Council drifted towards amphibious war. Even when the naval attack was sanctioned on 28th January there was no idea of supporting it with large military forces. Later on, when it was decided to mass troops in the neighbourhood of the Dardanelles with a view to assisting further operations when once the fleet had forced a passage, Lord Kitchener impressed upon Sir Ian Hamilton that the army should be made clearly to understand that they were second string, and were not to take an active part unless the Admiralty found they were unable to carry the plan through unaided. Unfortunately, however, the Admiralty did not leave the hornets' nest alone until they had kicked it over.

The writer contends that, if the various expeditionary forces which were sent from India in 1914 to different theatres had been amalgamated, organised into four divisions and flung on to the Gallipoli Peninsula at the earliest possible moment after the bombardment of Odessa, the Great War would have been over in the spring of 1915. At first sight this may appear to be a sweeping statement, but an attempt will be made to show that at all events it is not inconsistent with facts, and, further, that such a decision might have been arrived at without borrowing from the wisdom which is the product of after-knowledge.

Now in order to make what follows as clear as possible, it will be necessary to show the dispositions of the Turkish Army on the day Turkey came into the war. These details are set out in the subjoined table, which was prepared at the Turkish Ministry of War :—

European Turkey	7 divisions.
Western Asia Minor	9 ,,
Eastern Asia Minor	9 ,,
Syria and Palestine	5 ,,
Hejaz, Yemen, and Asir	4 ,,
Mesopotamia	4 ,,
Total	38 divisions

There were also five divisions in the early stages of formation, but these cannot be taken into account. It will therefore be observed that when Turkey entered the lists *three-quarters of her entire army was in Asia*. In the Gallipoli Peninsula itself there was only a portion of one division ;

this was the 9th, and its headquarters were at Chanak, on the Asiatic side.   Those landing-places on the peninsula which by the following April had been converted into veritable death-traps were in November entirely undefended and unoccupied. If, therefore, the amalgamated Indian Expeditionary Forces had been sent to the Gallipoli Peninsula in November 1914, it is highly probable that they could have landed without a single shot being fired.   If there had been any opposition at all it could only have been very slight, and could not possibly have saved Sari Bair, the Kilid Bahr plateau, and Achi Baba from immediate capture. With these three key positions in our hands, the Dardanelles forts, which are entirely commanded by them, would have been obliged to surrender, whereupon the allied fleets could have passed up the straits at once.

It is important to note that the only Turkish troops which could have been employed to oppose our advance from the beach were those actually in the peninsula at the time, namely, the bulk of one division.   As regards Turkish reinforcements, practically only those troops who were already on the European side would have been available against us, because the command of the Sea of Marmara would have passed into our hands before arrangements could have been made to transport them across from any of the large garrison centres, with the possible exception of Panderma.   Moreover, our troops at Anzac or Suvla would have been very much closer to the Bulair lines than any of the Turkish divisions, as will be seen from the following table, which shows the dispositions of the Turkish forces *in Europe* on the 1st November 1914 :—

Division.			Station.
1st	.	.	. Constantinople.
2nd	.	.	. Hademkeui.
3rd	.	.	. Constantinople.
4th	.	.	. Adrianople.
5th	.	.	. Adrianople.
6th	.	.	. Kirk Kilisse.
7th	.	.	. Rodosto.

About this time there were six Turkish divisions in transit as follows :—Two divisions were *en route* to Panderma from Denizli and Konia ; two to the Black Sea littoral ; and two to Constantinople from Kaiserie and Adana. Even assuming that a regiment or two could have been brought across from Panderma in time, and also that some of the troops in transit could have been diverted to Constantinople, it is difficult to see how more than eleven Turkish divisions could have been concentrated in Europe before the Turks lost the command of the Sea of Marmara. When once that was gone, all movements by sea would cease.

It must also be remembered that at this time the Turks were very anxious about the attitude of Bulgaria and Greece, and consequently that they were obliged to keep a considerable force to watch their western frontier. This alone immobilised four divisions, whilst at least one other was required for garrison duties in and round the capital. Therefore the maximum striking force immediately available against the peninsula would have been six divisions.

There are some authorities who consider that, had it not been for the operations in the Dardanelles, Bulgaria would have joined the Central Powers at a much earlier date. There are others again, whose opinions are equally entitled to respect, who declare that Bulgaria was on the point of coming in against Turkey early in 1915, and that they would certainly have done so at once if we had forced the Dardanelles.

It can be safely asserted that with the allied fleets in the Sea of Marmara and in the Gulf of Saros, the Bulair lines could have been easily held against such a force as this. The Bulair lines, in fact, are only tenable by the power which has the command of the environing seas, and it is only necessary to glance at the map to see what a hopeless task it would have been for the Turks to have attacked them, with our ships strung out along both shores of the narrow isthmus, and taking the Turkish line of advance in both flanks at close ranges for several miles.

With the command of the Sea of Marmara in our hands the Turkish Army would have been virtually cut in two, and all their divisions on the Caucasus, Egyptian, and Mesopotamian fronts would have been in the air, with no line of supply. Moreover, a line of communication with Russia would have been opened up, and that alone might have turned the scales of war.

It is a matter of history that Germany and Austria began to throw out feelers for peace in January 1915. With Turkey down and out in the first round, how long would they have dared to carry on the conflict alone?

CHAPTER IX

THE REBELLION IN OMAN

No sooner had the combined operations in Tangistan been concluded than affairs in Oman took an unfavourable turn.

During the latter part of May 1913 reports from Nizwa and Rustaq began to reach His Highness Faisal bin Turki bin Said, Sultan of Oman, to the effect that a serious rising was being organised under the ringleadership of the principal Ibadhi sheikh, Abdullah bin Hamid-as-Salimi, an old and half-blind man, who was about to proclaim a *jihad* with the object of setting up his son-in-law, Salim bin Rashid-al-Kharusi, as Imam of the Muslims of Oman in the place of the Sultan on account of the alleged leanings of the latter towards foreign governments and institutions. The rebellious faction included practically the whole of the large tribal confederacies known as the Ghafiri and the Hinawi. Two other prominent figures were Isa bin Salih-al-Harithi, an influential Hinawiyah sheikh ; and Hamyar bin Nasir-an-Nabhani, sheikh of the Bani Riyam, the tribe in which the rebellion started.

For many years before the Great War Muscat had been the centre of the arms traffic in the Persian Gulf. To put the matter briefly, these arms were brought from Hamburg, Antwerp, Djiboutil, and other places by steamer and landed in Muscat, whence the great bulk of them were carried across in dhows to the Mekran coast. From a hundred coves and creeks along that shore they were sent on donkeys and camels to the various dumps inland in a continual stream of small consignments. They were then taken away by *kafila* to the Helmund, whence they found their way into Afghanistan and the tribal country on the north-west frontier of India.

In order to check this traffic in arms, which by the year 1909 had increased so enormously as to cause the Government of India grave concern, an agreement was entered into with the Sultan of Oman by which a bonded warehouse was to be established in Muscat for all arms and ammunition landed at that port. It was the institution of this bonded warehouse system that stamped out the gun-running in the Persian Gulf. In return for his valuable co-operation and assistance in this matter the Sultan was granted a suitable subsidy. This strangling of the arms traffic, however, deprived a large number of his subjects of a means of livelihood that was at once agreeable and lucrative, and created a situation of discontent which the old Sheikh Abdullah exploited to the fullest advantage.

The troubles were started in Tanuf, a small village lying cramped up under some cliffs nearly a hundred miles from Muscat as the crow flies, and during the third week of May the rebels threatened the towns of Nizwa and Rustaq. On 27th May some of the Sultan's topchis left Muscat to join Saiyid Nadir, his second son, at Bidbid, which is a little more than twenty-one miles inland from

the port of Sib. Shortly afterwards Nizwa, reputed
to be the strongest fort in Oman, fell owing to the
treachery of the inhabitants of the Muddah quarter,
who allowed the Imam's men to enter, not, however, without resistance from the loyal party under
the Wali, who shot himself.

Early in June Saiyid Nadir advanced from
Bidbid with 2000 men and established himself at
Hisn Samail, a strong fort nearly twenty-one miles
higher up the valley. A few days later the Sultan's
yacht *Nur-al-Bahr* arrived at Muscat with about
500 Shihuhs from Khasab, in the Ruus-al-Jibal.
I have rarely seen natives of so wild and startled
an appearance, or in such a backward state of
civilisation ; they growled and chattered over their
food like animals. They were sent off almost at
once to Sib, where they disembarked for Samail.
About this time we received news that the fort of
Izki—often called Zikki—had fallen into the hands
of the Imam. On June 20th fighting occurred at
Awabi in which Saiyid bin Rashid, an influential
sheikh and supporter of the Imam, was killed.
Four days later Awabi fell, and with it, Bait Awabi,
a fort of great natural strength. The Imam and
Isa bin Salih were now at Izki, and on June 29th
600 of the Bani Bu Ali tribe from Ja'alan, under
Muhammad bin Nasir, a nephew of the old sheikh,
arrived at Bidbid. The Sultan would not allow
the Bani Bu Ali to advance beyond that place,
because if they went on to Samail there would be
a danger of their being cut off by a force advancing
down the Wadi-al-Aqq, whereas Bidbid was below
the junction of the two routes leading down to
Muscat. On July 6th, however, the Bani Bu Ali
returned to Muscat without orders, thus leaving
the road into the capital open.

Prior to 1915, the Bani Bu Ali were the only tribe of the Oman Sultanate who had met a British force. On the 9th November 1820 they defeated a force of British Indian sepoys at their village of Balad Bani Bu Ali, and on the 2nd March 1821 they suffered severe retribution near the same place. The Royal Dublin Fusiliers, some half-dozen Indian infantry regiments, and the 3rd Royal Sappers and Miners, all bear the battle-honour " Beni Boo Alli."

There was considerable alarm in the bazaar when it became known that the Imam had advanced to Izki, and with a view to allaying the popular excitement the Sultan asked the Indian Government to send troops to his assistance. The request was granted, and on July 9th Lieutenant-Colonel F. A. Smith, commanding the troops in the Persian Gulf, and 256 men of the 2nd Q.V.O. Rajputs under Major F. P. S. Dunsford, arrived at Muscat from Bushire by the fast mail.[1] The same steamer took them round to Matrah, where they disembarked at once. They camped for the night at Jabru, and the following morning they were visited by His Highness the Sultan and his third son, Saiyid Hamud, who were accompanied by Major S. G. Knox, the Political Agent at Muscat, Commanders Hill, Mellor, and Ballard, and the naval and military intelligence officer.

It will be recollected that the town of Muscat, which is the capital of the Oman Sultanate, is completely shut in by rugged hills, rendering it almost inaccessible from the land side. In fact the only practicable line of communication between

[1] The other British officers with this detachment were :—
Captain W. R. C. Griffith (Adjutant) ; Lieutenant C. D. Noyes ; and Captain W. L. Watson, I.M.S.

central Oman and the capital runs through Matrah,
and thence by sea.   In view of the circumstance
that all the caravan routes from the interior con-
verge at Ruwi, four or five miles from the coast,
any advance on Matrah would have to be made
from the direction of that village, and it was therefore decided to post the Indian troops somewhere
between these two places.   A large defensible
house, known as Bait-al-Falaj, was selected as the
headquarters of the detachment and handed over
to the military authorities.   It was the property
of the Sultan's eldest son, and was conveniently
situated in the open plain behind Matrah.   The
heat during the summer was very great and the
incidence of disease somewhat high.

On July 18th the Sultan went to Sib in his yacht,
and the next day the Political Agent and myself
followed in H.M.S. *Philomel.*   Sib is a small
scattered town on the Batinah coast, about five-
and-twenty miles west of Muscat.   On arrival
there we proceeded to the Wali's house, which was
situated on the left bank of the Wadi Samail.
After a long conversation with the Sultan, which
was chiefly about God and to-morrow, we returned
to Muscat.

The next evening during dinner two Arab
messengers rushed into the Agency with a letter
from Saiyid Taimur, who had just arrived in
Matrah from Sib in the *Nur-al-Bahr*.   The letter
contained the report that Sib was to be attacked
that night.   We left the Agency at once and
hurried off to Matrah in a steam pinnace.   On
arrival there we called upon Saiyid Taimur in the
Nur-al-Bahr, and he assured us that an attack on
Sib was imminent.   After a hurried interview we
returned to Muscat, embarked in the *Alert*, and

left at midnight for Sib. We anchored at dawn, and at 6 a.m. Major Knox, Commander Wood, and myself went off to see the Sultan. We failed to discover any justification for the alarming scare of the night before ; in fact the question of an attack on Sib was not even mentioned.

The *Alert* remained at Sib till the following day. It was a dead calm tropical night, and the combination of heat and moisture inside that little sloop was almost unbearable. With a wet-bulb reading of 96°, the climate can scarcely be imagined or described. We returned to Muscat on July 23rd, and two days later left for Sohar with a letter from the Sultan to the Wali. The town of Sohar lies about one hundred and ten miles by sea to the westward of Muscat ; it contains several hundred houses, and a huge, square, four-storeyed fort, very dilapidated. We stayed there long enough to make a useful reconnaissance of the place.

At the end of July Samail fell owing to the treachery of its defenders. All opposition to the rebels, as far as the forces of the Sultan were concerned, was now at an end, and it was only the presence of the Rajputs and the navy ships that prevented Matrah and Muscat from sharing the same fate as Samail. The Sultan, however, did not dare to use either of these instruments of a foreign power unless his capital was actually threatened, which in the circumstances was not likely. Saiyids Taimur and Nadir returned to Muscat on 11th August amidst the firings of guns and other unmerited welcomings. The first game between the Sultan and the Imam thus ended in a stalemate.

In the following November the 2nd Rajputs

were relieved by the 102nd K.E.O. Grenadiers. The rebellion still dragged on, but nothing definite occurred until the news of the Great War began to filter through, and then it took a new lease of life. The Germans in the Persian Gulf soon began to exploit the unrest in Oman, and to turn it to good account. They got into touch with the agitators there, as they were doing in Tangistan, with the object of persuading the rebels to attack us. They left no stone unturned to find a means of immobilising allied troops, no matter where or how few they might be.

In December 1914 persistent reports kept coming in to the effect that the Imam and his lieutenants, Isa bin Salih and Hamyar, were collecting men with the intention of attacking Matrah and Muscat. The officer commanding the troops in Oman was now Colonel S. M. Edwardes,[1] who had under him his own regiment, the 102nd Grenadiers, and also the 95th Russell's Infantry, commanded by Major F. F. Major. Although the rebels had been threatening to attack for the past eighteen months, it now looked as if they really meant business at last. The situation began to develop rapidly ; it was evident that there were fresh influences at work.

There was now occasional sniping at the pickets at night. On the 7th January 1915 there was reported to be a gathering of some 300 men at Mutahaddamat, about six miles from Ruwi. The village of Wataiyah (5½ miles from Matrah) was raided on the 8th ; and on the 9th firing was heard in the hills beyond that settlement. On the 10th a small party of men mounted on camels was seen approaching Wataiyah, and the news was received

[1] Now Brigadier-General S. M. Edwardes, C.B., C.M.G., D.S.O.

that the Imam and Hamyar were close at hand in the Wadi Boshar, and Isa at Khuwair, a hamlet eight miles west of Matrah.   At the same time it was reported that a force was debouching from Ghubrah on Wataiyah with four standards, and another at Quram with six standards.   Messages from the outposts continued to come in of an increasing force of rebels concentrating at Wataiyah.

In order to protect the town of Matrah, Colonel Edwardes had arranged with the Sultan that a section of the outpost line nearest the sea should be taken over by the Sultan's forces, of whom about five hundred had recently returned from Quryat where they had been engaging the Bani Battash.   These men belonged to the Bani Amr tribe from the Batinah coast.   They refused to leave the walls of Matrah, no doubt hoping for better things later on if the fighting got close to the town.   A small Arab picket was on the hills west of Darsait, but they ran away when firing commenced.   Another picket of fifteen of the Sultan's Baluchis was said to be on the Aqabat Aiyint.   This was all the protection Matrah had if the rebels held the Indian infantry and marched on that town.

On the night of the 10th–11th it was dark from 6.30 p.m. till 2 a.m., when there was a faint moon. Ten minutes later a tremendous fusillade opened on the picket line, especially against the right of of the 102nd Grenadiers, where after two hours' fighting the picket was driven in.   At 6.30 a.m. Major A. C. Edwardes, with as many fit men as could be collected, and two machine-guns, was ordered out to clear the hills and retake the lost picket-post.   The frontal attack advanced towards a point known as Red Hill, and soon came under fire. Captain S. B. Coates, who was in command, was wounded but continued to advance. Having gained Red Hill they pushed on by regular stages, keeping up a brisk fire to assist the development and progress of the flank attack, which had moved out under command of Major Edwardes towards the centre of the 102nd Grenadiers' picket line. One by one the various ridges and passes were cleared, the enemy losing heavily and those retiring being hurried along by the approach of the 95th regiment towards Sadd Ruwi. When the flank attack had wheeled to the right up on to the high ground, Major Pratt with a platoon of the 95th joined in on the left and assisted in the advance. The total strength of the enemy must have been nearly 3000, but in spite of these numbers and the difficult nature of the ground, they were defeated with losses estimated at 300, the rebel chief Isa bin Salih being wounded and his brother killed. Our own casualties were slight, most of them occurring amongst the 102nd Grenadiers.

The orders issued to Colonel Edwardes were that he was not to advance, but if attacked to inflict as much loss upon the enemy as possible. It must have afforded him and the troops engaged the utmost satisfaction to have been able to carry out those orders so successfully.

CHAPTER X

I shall go down in history as the man who demonstrated the vulnerability of the British fleet. Unless they bring a large army with them they will be caught in a trap. It seems to me a foolish enterprise.—ENVER PASHA, 15th *March* 1915.

IN this chapter it is proposed to show the composition, organisation, and strength of the Turkish Army in Gallipoli at certain selected times, namely, (1) on the day of the general mobilisation of the Turkish Army, (2) at the landing, (3) during the August offensives, (4) at the evacuation, and (5) when the armistice with Turkey was signed.

The information given in the following pages was obtained entirely from Turkish sources, and no British, French, German, or other publication has been consulted. The *Order of Battle* of the Turkish Army during the August offensives calls for special comment, as it was translated from the *original* order of battle which was prepared for and used by the Chief of the Staff of the Gallipoli army and lent by him to the author. It was a work of art in itself, the different units being shown by means of conventional signs, all beautifully executed in various colours on tracing silk, with the description and details of each minutely written beneath it in Turkish. The information

contained in this historical document is of great
value.

The five headings given above may now be
dealt with in turn.

(1) THE GENERAL MOBILISATION OF THE TURKISH ARMY

When the imperial *irade* for the general mobilisation of the Turkish Army came into effect there
was only a portion of one division in the whole of
the Gallipoli Peninsula.   This was the 9th Division,
belonging to the 3rd Army Corps which had its
headquarters at Chanak, and consisted of the 25th,
26th, and 27th Regiments.   Each of these is
definitely stated to have had three battalions,
which is worthy of note, because the 1st/26th Regiment was then in Basrah, and took a leading part
in all the early operations in Mesopotamia, its last
remnants being destroyed at Barjisiyah with the
1st Muretteb Battalion.   When the 1st/26th was
sent to Mesopotamia and lent to the 13th Army
Corps it must have been regarded, with strange
prescience, as being finally lost to the 9th Division,
for a fourth battalion was evidently raised to take
its place.

It should be noted that the orders for general
mobilisation were issued at the beginning of
August 1914, so that by the time Turkey entered
the lists the mobilisation of her army had been in
progress for very nearly three months.

(2) AT THE LANDING

From the outset the Turks knew that sooner or
later the Allies would strike a blow at the vital
parts of their empire, namely, the Dardanelles.

All they could hope was that the British and French would defer their attack until the fine weather had set in. There were Turkish officers at the Ministry of War who regarded our occupation of Basrah merely as a ruse to draw troops away from Constantinople. Conversely, their own attack on the Suez Canal was devised partly with the idea of immobilising British troops in Egypt. Even when the allied fleets were repulsed on the 18th March, it was thought they would return with troops. So on the 25th March 1915 the Fifth Army was raised with the special object of providing a powerful force for the defence of the Dardanelles. The importance attached to the project may be judged from the fact that the nucleus of the force included no less than five pre-war divisions. Turkish mobilisation, however, could not make much headway against the current of battle and disease, and the formation of the Fifth Army had not greatly progressed when, on the 25th April—that is to say, exactly a month after its inception,—it was called upon to oppose the Allies' landing.

About that time Turkish troops were continually arriving in the peninsula, but there were no records in the Ministry of War to show what units or portions of units had arrived at any selected moment. For instance, the author was given an order of battle which was said to be that of the Fifth Army at the time of the landing, but on investigation it proved to have been made out some time before that event and had not been corrected up to the 25th April. I find I have endorsed the document with the following remark :—" I have not been able to identify the units that opposed the Anzac landing, but they appear to have been Corps troops of the equivalent of a division, be-

longing to the 3rd Army Corps." The Turkish
General Staff informed me that "before the
landing" there were 62,077 combatants in the
Gallipoli army.

As the Allies' ships in the Gulf of Saros could
enfilade the Bulair lines, the Turks left them
practically unoccupied, but two divisions were
kept in reserve near the isthmus in case of a landing
there. Both these divisions were posted on the
east coast of Gallipoli, one on each side of the
Bulair lines ; the 5th was at Sharkeui on the Sea
of Marmara, well out of range of our guns, and the
7th was just outside the town of Gallipoli, where
only the fifteen-inch guns of the *Queen Elizabeth*
could reach them.

The order of battle at the landing was as
follows :—

European Side

3RD ARMY CORPS

7th Division.—In reserve outside Gallipoli town.

9th Division.—Helles area.

19th Division.—Maidos, and along the Boghali
road.

Corps Troops.—The equivalent of a division, on
the west coast of the peninsula.

NOT BELONGING TO ANY ARMY CORPS

5th Division.—In reserve at Sharkeui, on the
Sea of Marmara.

Independent Cavalry Brigade.—Strung out along
the coast of the Gulf of Saros from Examil [1] to
Enos.

[1] On some maps this place is shown as Hexamil or Hexamili,
eight miles north-east from Bulair village.

Asiatic Side

15TH ARMY CORPS

3rd and 11th Divisions.—Round Kum Kale and the village of Yeni Shehr.

(3) THE AUGUST OFFENSIVE

On the 3rd August 1914 the Turkish Army consisted of thirty-eight divisions, namely, the 1st to the 18th and the 21st to the 40th. Very few of them had been kept up to their peace establishments, and therefore many thousands of men were required to bring them on to a war footing. During the war a further twenty-five regular and seven Caucasus divisions were formed, yet so great was the wastage that the Turkish Army at no time consisted of more than forty-three divisions.

In August 1915—that is to say, a year after the general mobilisation—the Turkish Army consisted of forty-one divisions, with seven others in process of formation. A scrutiny of the subjoined order of battle will show that the forces then in Gallipoli (the number of combatants in which had been more than doubled since the first landing) amounted to about one-half of the Turkish Army, and included the whole of the famous old Constantinople, Adrianople, and Gallipoli Army Corps, as well as those of Smyrna, Angora, and Aleppo. In addition to all these crack divisions there were four battalions of the " Fire-Extinguishing Regiment," which is probably the best fighting regiment in the Ottoman Army. There was also a large number of German officers and men, and some of the coast batteries were manned by picked German bluejackets from the *Goeben* and *Breslau*. Taken as a whole, therefore, the army in Gallipoli may be justly considered to have been the finest that has ever taken the field in the history of the Turkish Empire. There could be no comparison between it and the Yildirim army which was opposed to Lord Allenby in Palestine in 1918.

ORDER OF BATTLE OF THE ARMY IN GALLIPOLI, AUGUST 1915

FIFTH ARMY

G.O.C.-in-C. . . Marshal Liman Von Sanders.
Chief of Staff . Colonel Kiazim Bey.[1]

1ST ARMY CORPS

1ST DIVISION.—Regiments . 70th 71st 124th
　　　　　　　　Battalions . . 3 3 3
　　　　　　　　Machine-Gun Coys. 1 1 ..
　　　Cavalry.—1st squadron, 5th Cavalry Regiment.
　　　Artillery.—1st Artillery Regiment—4 Field Batteries, 2 Mountain Batteries.
　1 Company Engineers, and 1 Field Hospital.

2ND DIVISION.—Regiments . . 1st 5th 6th
　　　　　　　　Battalions . . 3 3 3
　　　　　　　　Machine-Gun Coys. 1 .. ..
　　　Cavalry.—2nd Squadron, 5th Cavalry Regiment.
　　　Artillery.—2nd Artillery Regiment—4 Field Batteries.
　1 Company Engineers, 1 Signal Section, 1 Pontoon Section, 1 Field Hospital.

[1] Afterwards Major-General Kiazim Pasha, Deputy Chief of the General Staff.

3RD DIVISION.—Regiments. . 31st 32nd 39th
                 Battalions   .   3   3   3
                 Machine-Gun Coys. ..   1   ..
   Cavalry.—2nd Squadron, 3rd Cavalry Regiment.
   Artillery.—3rd Artillery Regiment—2 Field Batteries.
   1 Company Engineers, 1 Signal Section, 1 Field Hospital.

CORPS TROOPS.—Signal Section.

2ND ARMY CORPS

4TH DIVISION.—Regiments . 10th 11th 12th
                 Battalions . . 4   4   4
                 Machine-Gun Coys. 1   1   0
   Cavalry.—1st Squadron, 3rd Cavalry Regiment.
   Artillery.—4th Artillery Regiment—5 Field Batteries.
   1 Company Engineers, 1 Signal Section, 1 Field Hospital.

5TH DIVISION.—Regiments . 13th 14th 15th
                 Battalions . . 3   3   3
                 Machine-Gun Coys. 1   1   1
   Cavalry.—3rd Squadron, 3rd Cavalry Regiment.
   Artillery.—5th Artillery Regiment—4 Field Batteries, 2 Mountain Batteries.
   1 Company Engineers, 1 Signal Section, 1 Pontoon Section, 1 Field Hospital.

6TH DIVISION.—Regiments . 16th 17th 18th
                 Battalions . . 4   4   4
                 Machine-Gun Coys. 1   1   1

Cavalry.—5th Squadron, 3rd Cavalry Regiment.

Artillery.—6th Artillery Regiment—4 Field
Batteries, 2 Mountain Batteries.

CORPS TROOPS.—4th Squadron, 3rd Cavalry Regiment; 1 Company Engineers, 1 Signal Section.

3RD ARMY CORPS

7TH DIVISION.—Regiments   . 19th 20th 21st
　　　　　　　　Battalions .   . 3   3   3
　　　　　　　　Machine-Gun Coys. 1   ..   1

Cavalry.—2nd Squadron, 4th Cavalry Regiment.

Artillery.—7th Artillery Regiment—4 Field
Batteries, 2 Mountain Batteries.

1 Company Engineers, 1 Field Hospital.

8TH DIVISION.—Regiments.   . 22nd 23rd 24th
　　　　　　　　Battalions   . 3   3   3
　　　　　　　　Machine-Gun Coys. 1   1   1 [1]

Cavalry.—3rd Squadron, 4th Cavalry Regiment.

Artillery.—8th Artillery Regiment—4 Field
Batteries, 2 Mountain Batteries.

1 Company Engineers, 1 Field Hospital.

9TH DIVISION.—Regiments   . 25th 26th 27th
　　　　　　　　Battalions .   . 3   3   3
　　　　　　　　Machine-Gun Coys. 1   1 [1] 1

Cavalry.—4th Squadron, 4th Cavalry Regiment.

Artillery.—9th Artillery Regiment—4 Field
Batteries, 2 Mountain Batteries.

1 Company Engineers, 1 Field Hospital.

[1] Captured from British.

CORPS TROOPS.—1st Squadron, 4th Cavalry Regiment; 1 Signal Section, 1 Company Engineers, 2 Pontoon Sections.

5TH ARMY CORPS

13TH DIVISION.—Regiments . . 4th 46th 60th
Battalions . . 4   4   4
Machine-Gun Coys. 1   ..   ..
Cavalry.—1st Squadron, 11th Cavalry Regiment.
Artillery.—13th Artillery Regiment—4 Field Batteries, 2 Mountain Batteries (not Q.F.).
1 Company Engineers, 1 Field Hospital.

14TH DIVISION.—Regiments . 41st 42nd 55th
Battalions . 4   4   4
Machine-Gun Coys. 1   ..   1
Cavalry.—2nd Squadron, 11th Cavalry Regiment.
Artillery.—14th Artillery Regiment—4 Field Batteries, 1 Mountain Battery (not Q.F.).
1 Company Engineers, 1 Field Hospital.

15TH DIVISION.—Regiments . 38th 45th 56th
Battalions . 4   4   4
Machine-Gun Coys. 1 [1]   1   ..
Cavalry.—6th Squadron, 11th Cavalry Regiment.
Artillery.—15th Artillery Regiment—4 Field Batteries, 2 Mountain Batteries (not Q.F.).
1 Company Engineers, 1 Signal Section, 1 Field Hospital.

[1] Captured from British.

CORPS TROOPS.—4th Squadron, 11th Cavalry Regiment; 1 Company Engineers, 1 Signal Section.

6th ARMY CORPS

24TH DIVISION.—

Regiments	. 2nd	58th	143rd
Battalions	. 4	4	4
Machine-Gun Coys.	1	..	..

Cavalry.—2nd Squadron, 27th Cavalry Regiment.

Artillery.—24th Artillery Regiment—4 Field Batteries, 2 Mountain Batteries (not Q.F.).

1 Company Engineers, 1 Field Hospital.

26TH DIVISION.—

Regiments	. 59th	76th	78th
Battalions	. 4	4	4
Machine-Gun Coys.	..	1	1

Cavalry.—3rd Squadron, 27th Cavalry Regiment.

Artillery.—26th Artillery Regiment—2 Field Batteries, 2 Mountain Batteries (not Q.F.).

1 Company Engineers, 1 Signal Section.

CORPS TROOPS.—4th Squadron, 27th Cavalry Regiment; 1 Mountain Battery, 1 Company Engineers, 1 Signal Section.

DIVISIONS NOT ALLOCATED TO AN ARMY CORPS

10TH DIVISION.—

Regiments	. 28th	29th	30th
Battalions	. 3	3	3
Machine-Gun Coys.	1	1	..

Cavalry.—None.

Artillery.—10th Artillery Regiment—4 Field Batteries.

1 Company Engineers, 1 Field Hospital.

11TH DIVISION.—Regiments . 33rd 126th 127th
                Battalions . 3 3 3
                Machine-Gun Coys. 1 0 1 [1]
    Cavalry.—2nd Squadron, 12th Cavalry Regiment.
    Artillery.—11th Artillery Regiment—4 Field Batteries, 2 Mountain Batteries
  1 Company Engineers, 1 Signal Section, 1 Field Hospital.

12TH DIVISION.—Regiments . 34th 35th 36th
                Battalions . 4 4 4
                Machine-Gun Coys... .. 1
    Cavalry.—4th Squadron, 12th Cavalry Regiment.
    Artillery.—12th Artillery Regiment—4 Field Batteries.
  1 Company Engineers, 1 Field Hospital.

16TH DIVISION.—Regiments . 47th 48th 125th
                Battalions . 3 3 3
                Machine-Gun Coys. .. 1 [1] 1 [2]
    Cavalry.—1st Squadron, 27th Cavalry Regiment.
    Artillery.—16th Artillery Regiment—2 Field Batteries, 2 Mountain Batteries (not Q.F.).
  1 Company Engineers, 1 Signal Section, 1 Field Hospital.

19TH DIVISION.—Regiments . 57th 72nd 77th
                Battalions . 3 3 3
                Machine-Gun Coys. 1 2 [3] ..
    Cavalry.—5th Squadron, 4th Cavalry Regiment.

[1] Captured from British.   [2] Hotchkiss.
[3] One Hotchkiss and 1 Maxim captured from British.

Artillery.—39th Artillery Regiment—2 Field Batteries, 2 Field Batteries (not Q.F.), 2 Mountain Batteries.

1 Company Engineers, 1 Field Hospital.

20TH DIVISION.—

Regiments	. 61st	62nd	63rd
Battalions	. 4	4	4
Machine-Gun Coys.	1	..	..

Cavalry.—3rd Squadron, 12th Regiment.

Artillery.—20th Artillery Regiment—4 Field Batteries.

1 Company Engineers, 1 Field Hospital.

25TH DIVISION.—

Regiments	. 73rd	74th	75th
Battalions	. 4	4	4
Machine-Gun Coys.	1	..	..

Cavalry.—1st Squadron, 29th Cavalry Regiment.

Artillery.—25th Artillery Regiment—2 Field Batteries.

1 Company Engineers, 1 Signal Section, 1 Field Hospital.

42ND DIVISION.—

Regiments	. 65th	66th	123rd
Battalions	. 4	4	4
Machine-Gun Coys.	..	1	..

Cavalry.—1st Squadron, 12th Cavalry Regiment.

Artillery.—42nd Artillery Regiment—3 Field Batteries (not Q.F.), 3 Mountain Batteries (not Q.F.).

1 Company Engineers, 1 Signal Section.

INDEPENDENT CAVALRY BRIGADE

1st Lancers with a Machine-Gun Company.
7th Cavalry Regiment.

13th Cavalry Regiment with a Machine-Gun Company.

Battery of Horse Artillery.

1 Engineers Section. 1 Field Hospital.

The following army corps and divisions are shown in Kiazim Pasha's order of battle as belonging to the Second Army :—5th Army Corps (13th and 14th Divisions), 14th Army Corps (8th and 10th Divisions), 15th Army Corps (3rd and 11th Divisions), 16th Army Corps (5th and 16th Divisions), 17th Army Corps (15th and 25th Divisions). For administrative purposes, however, the Second Army was merged in the Fifth Army, and therefore I have shown all units as belonging to the latter.

Army Troops of the Fifth Army

64th Regiment—3 battalions, 1 Machine-Gun Company.[1]

136th Regiment [2]—4 battalions.

The Gallipoli Gendarme Battalion.

,, Broussa ,, ,,

,, Karasi ,, ,,

,, Dardanelles ,, ,,

Constantinople Fire-Extinguishing Regiment— 4 battalions, namely, the 1st, 3rd, 5th, and 6th.

Adrianople Fortress Engineer Battalion—4 companies.

German Engineer Company.

3 Field Batteries (not Q.F.).

[1] Captured from the British. In 1916 this regiment joined the 14th Division.

[2] The 136th Regiment subsequently went to the 53rd Division.

1 platoon of Muhafiz Infantry.
2 troops of Muhafiz Cavalry.
1 Signal Company.
1 Wireless Section.
1 Flying Corps Company.

(4) THE EVACUATION

By the time the British evacuation began, the strength of the Fifth Army had dwindled to 138,879 of all ranks. The order of battle given under the present heading shows the Turkish forces in Gallipoli immediately after the evacuation of Anzac and Suvla, but before the transfer of divisions to the Southern, or Sedd-el-Bahr, Group. About this time seven Turkish divisions were sent away from the peninsula, one before and the remainder immediately after the Anzac and Suvla evacuations. Six others were transferred from the Anafarta and Northern Groups to the Southern Group as soon as the west coast was found to be clear of British troops.

The divisions sent out of the peninsula were the 2nd, 3rd, 4th, 5th, 10th, 13th, and 26th. It is instructive to note where these divisions were sent. The 2nd went to the Sixth Army in Mesopotamia; the 3rd, to the Fourth Army on the Turco-Egyptian frontier; the 4th, 5th, and 10th went to the Second Army in the Caucasus; the 13th was sent to quell the Kurdish rebellion in Dersim; and the 26th went to the Dobruja front.

Soon after the final evacuation, six more divisions, namely, the 1st, 7th, 8th, 9th, 11th, and 12th, were sent to the Caucasus; one more, the 6th, went to Mesopotamia; one more, the 14th, to Egypt; two more, the 15th and 25th, to the

Dobruja front; the 16th, to Panderma and Smyrna; the 19th, to Keshan and then to Galicia; the 20th, to Keshan; the 24th, to Chanak; whilst the 42nd joined the 14th Army Corps.

As we have already seen, the operations in Gallipoli had immobilised through many eventful months more than half the Turkish Army, and, moreover, incomparably the better half. The question of the Turkish losses in the peninsula was raised by the author in Constantinople at the end of 1918; after exhaustive investigation Javad Pasha informed me that the total casualties in the Gallipoli Army were estimated at 2160 officers and nearly 287,000 other ranks. In view of the fact that the incidence of disease, especially typhus and dysentery, was low, these figures are astounding and demonstrate more clearly than any words the severe character of the fighting. One can therefore readily appreciate the deep sense of relief which, in spite of the great opportunities they had allowed to slip through their fingers, the Turks undoubtedly felt when they realised we were preparing to evacuate the peninsula.

The following is an order of battle of the Fifth Army after the Anzac and Suvla evacuations, but before the transfer of divisions to the Sedd-el-Bahr area. In the course of compilation it was found that opinions at the Seraskerat were not unanimous on all points; nor was I able to identify satisfactorily the " unnumbered " division of the 3rd Army Corps.

Saros Group

17th Army Corps.—25th Division and Independent Cavalry Brigade. Watching the coast from the north of Suvla to Enos.

152 SOLDIERS OF THE PROPHET

Anafarta Group

15*th Army Corps.*—6th, 7th, and 8th Divisions.
16*th Army Corps.*—9th, 11th, and 12th Divisions.

Northern Group (Anzac)

3*rd Army Corps.*—16th and 19th Divisions and
one division unnumbered.

Southern Group (Sedd-el-Bahr)

14*th Army Corps.*—1st, 14th, 15th, and 20th
Divisions.

Asiatic Group

6*th Army Corps.*—24th and 42nd Divisions.
Watching the coast from Kum Kale to Gheyikli.

(5) THE SIGNING OF THE TURKISH ARMISTICE

The information under this heading is comparatively of little importance or interest. When the
author passed up the Dardanelles on the 6th
November 1918, three weak divisions, namely, the
49th, 55th, and the 60th, which then comprised
the 14th Army Corps, were in Gallipoli, and
nominally the headquarters of the Fifth Army were
there too. The 61st Division was strung out along
the Asiatic coast south of the straits. The famous
Fifth Army was finally disbanded on the 21st
November 1918, a fortnight after our arrival in
Constantinople.

CHAPTER XI

On the 28th September 1915 Major-General Townshend had at Kut brilliantly defeated a Turkish force of rather more than two divisions, a mounted brigade, and 38 guns under Nur-ed-Din Pasha. The British captured 1153 prisoners and 14 guns, and determined to follow up their success by advancing on Baghdad.

On 11th November El Kutuniyah was occupied by British advanced troops, and by 17th November the main portion of the British field force, consisting of the 6th (Poona) Division, the 30th Infantry Brigade, and the 6th Indian Cavalry Brigade, was concentrated there under the supreme command of General Sir John Nixon, who had placed the executive command in the hands of Major-General Townshend. The Turks, some 2000 strong with 4 guns, were holding an advanced position at Zeur, whilst their main position, held by three divisions and part of a fourth, a mounted brigade, and 38 guns, was astride the Tigris at Ctesiphon, with reserves at Qusaibah. On 19th November Zeur was occupied almost without opposition ; the Turks were taken by surprise at dawn and fell back on Ctesiphon. The British advance was continued to Lajj on the following day, and after a night march begun on the 21st General Townshend attacked the enemy at Ctesiphon on the morning of the 22nd.

The battle that ensued was a severe one ; it lasted all day, but could not be fought out owing to failing light.   Nevertheless the British succeeded in capturing the hostile position, and they bivouacked there for the night with 1300 prisoners in their hands.   The casualties on both sides were very heavy.   During the night of the 23rd–24th the Turks made a vigorous counter-attack which was repulsed.   The 24th and 25th were occupied in desultory fighting and in collecting wounded.   By the night of the 24th our information tended to show that the Turks were steadily retiring towards a line two miles east of Diyalah, which is about half-way between Ctesiphon and Baghdad, and that this line was strongly entrenched.   However, on the afternoon of the 25th, reliable reports were received from aeroplanes and patrols that the enemy were moving forward from Diyalah in two columns, one along the left bank of the Tigris and the other at turning distance inland, while a hostile cavalry brigade was threatening Bustan, about two miles south-east of Ctesiphon.   General Townshend rightly concluded that strong reinforcements had reached the enemy, and in order to avoid being pinned in he decided to retire to Lajj without delay.   This retirement was carried out with great skill during the night, but air reconnaissances conducted on the 26th and 27th revealed that the enemy were coming on in such force that General Townshend abandoned his intention of holding Lajj and retired to Aziziyah, which he reached unmolested during the night of the 27th–28th November.   From there the withdrawal was continued to Umm-at-Tubal, where the Turks attacked in great strength at daylight on the 1st December. They were, however, repulsed, and on 3rd December the British force reached Kut after one of the most successful retirements before greatly superior numbers that has ever been conducted, and which formed a fitting prelude to the siege with which the names of Kut and Townshend will ever be associated.

It was subsequently ascertained that the Turkish 18th Army Corps, whose staff had preceded it, began to arrive in Baghdad about the middle of October, and was hurried on down the Tigris at once. Owing to these reinforcements the Turkish superiority in numbers was now sufficiently great to enable them to surround the British, and by the evening of 7th December the investment of Kut was complete. Within two days the Turks worked round to Shaikh Sa'ad, some forty miles down the Tigris from Kut, and from that time onwards General Townshend's force was effectually cut off from the outer world.

It was a much-tried garrison that was now set the task of withstanding one of the most arduous sieges in the long annals of the British Army. The majority of the men had already fought for a year under extremely exhausting conditions, and the retirement from Ctesiphon had taxed their remaining strength to the utmost ; but there was no time to be lost if Kut was to be placed in a state of defence such as would enable the garrison to withstand the violent onslaughts which the Turks were sure to launch without delay. Only a few days were available, but they sufficed for the improvement of and addition to the existing works and trenches, and a series of determined assaults from the 8th to the 12th of December all ended in failure. Indeed, so dearly did the assailants pay for their ventures that they made no further efforts till Christmas, and thus gave General Townshend the opportunity he so much needed for the consolidation of his position, which he continued to improve as time went on.

During the night of December 23rd–24th, and throughout the 24th, heavy fire was concentrated on the Kut redoubt. The parapet was breached and the Turks effected an entrance, but they were driven out by a counter-attack and left a large number of dead behind them. However, the attacks were soon renewed, and throughout the night of the 24th–25th a fierce struggle took place round the redoubt. The enemy again effected a lodgment, but by morning they had been ejected and the assault, which must have cost them 2000 casualties, was finally defeated. After Christmas there were no further onslaughts of this kind, though bombardments and aerial bombings were frequent. As time went on the high-water season approached ; with the advent of April came the floods which forced both sides out of their forward trenches, leaving a broad tract of water-logged country between the opposing armies. Obviously such a state of affairs must have affected materially the Turkish plan of attack.

The squalid little town of Kut possessed few of the attributes essential to an improvised fortress of even moderate pretensions ; it had no resources apart from the traffic passing up and down the river, and the long line of communication between it and Basrah was rendered the more precarious owing to the difficulties of river transport and the unreliable character of the Arab tribes. Neverthe-

THE STORY OF KUT

less, the course of the Tigris where it passes Kut offered great advantages in that it formed a horse-shoe bend surrounding the town on three sides. This peculiarity of situation was turned to good account, and before long General Townshend had constructed formidable lines of works facing north-west between the two tips of the horse-shoe. These works were supplemented by others on the river front, and so skilfully were they all planned that the little garrison was able to keep out the Turks for nearly five months, and at the end of that time was no nearer defeat by force of arms than at the beginning.

The Turkish works round Kut consisted of chains of entrenchments and redoubts, enclosing the town on all sides. The three principal continuous lines extended across the north-west face at a radius of about three miles from Kut citadel, their flanks resting on the river. The Turkish advanced trenches were within bombing range of ours. To the west and south-west another line subtended the angle formed by the Tigris and the Hai, whilst to the south and east redoubts and other works ran round the river salient to Muhammad Abul Hasan. Downstream of Kut the Turks constructed successive lines of entrenchments extending roughly as far as the Wadi stream, with the object of preventing any relieving force from reaching the beleagured garrison.

Little time had been lost in getting this relieving force together, and the first important battle was fought on 6th January and the two following days at Shaikh Sa'ad, where two Turkish divisions and a mounted brigade, the whole aggregating about 15,000 men and 41 guns, were defeated by General Aylmer, and 512 prisoners with 12 officers and 2

mountain guns were captured. The Turks now
withdrew to Wadi, where they were again attacked
on 13th January and forced to retire on Umm-al-
Hannah, the first of the series of very strong
positions which they had been preparing to stop
our advance. Behind Umm-al-Hannah lay Falahiyah and Sanna'iyat, which latter became very
formidable. These positions owed their strength
to the fact that one flank rested on the Tigris and
the other on the broad Suwaicha marsh ; thus
they closed the narrow strip of comparatively
dry ground which lay in between. A somewhat
similar strip, though broader and less clearly
defined, extended between the Tigris and the Umm-
al-Brahm marsh, so that on both banks of the
river a frontal attack was the only course open to
the assailants. Behind the three positions already
mentioned lay a fourth, known as that of As-Sinn ;
it was about eight miles below Kut and stretched
from a point three miles north of the Suwaicha
marsh across the Tigris to the Dujailah redoubt,
on the canal of the same name, and was thence
prolonged by a line of six redoubts to the river Hai.

The first attack on Umm-al-Hannah was made
on January 20th, and though our troops gallantly
took the enemy's first line trenches, they were
driven out again by a strong counter-attack. The
offensive was not resumed for more than six weeks.
The chief reason for this delay was the abnormally
wet and stormy weather, which made the annual
floods worse than usual and rendered the country
in the theatre of operations almost impassable.
However, on 8th March General Aylmer made
another determined effort. He attempted to turn
the position at As-Sinn by a movement south of
the Tigris, and only just failed to take the Dujailah

redoubt ; but difficulties of supplies and the arrival of enemy reinforcements told too heavily against our troops, and the attempt had to be abandoned.

About the middle of March General Gorringe assumed command, and during the first week in April he began a series of operations for the relief of the Kut garrison, now hard pressed for want of food. On April 5th, Umm-al-Hannah, Abu Rumman, and Falahiyah all fell in rapid succession, but from the nature of the resistance it was evident that these positions had only been held lightly and that the bulk of the Turks had withdrawn. On 6th April and again on 9th April they were vigorously attacked at Sanna'iyat. On both days partial success was achieved, but no definite decision in our favour could be obtained. The next battle took place on the right bank of the river at Bait 'Isa on 16th April and the two following days. Our troops advanced 2000 yards and captured the hostile position, and though driven back half a mile by a series of counter-attacks launched in great strength against them during the night of the 17th–18th, they succeeded in holding the rest of the ground gained and in taking 415 prisoners with 13 officers. The British losses were heavy, but not as heavy as those of the Turks, of whom no less than 3100 dead were actually counted in front of our lines.

On 23rd April the position at Sanna'iyat was attacked for the third time, but owing to the floods the attack had to be made on a front of only three hundred yards. The casualties were very heavy, and though the first line of the enemy's trenches was stormed our troops were driven out again by strong counter-attacks. This was the last attempt made, and on 29th April Kut surrendered.

The story of the siege of Kut is one of the finest recorded in our history. For all but five long months General Townshend and his gallant troops held their own against enormous odds. They had suffered heavy losses before the investment began, and of course during the siege their numbers dwindled daily from shell-fire and disease. The question of food soon demanded attention and would have become acute at a much earlier date but for the discovery on 24th January of supplies of buried grain which provided the garrison for a long time with a moderate ration on a constantly decreasing scale. A civil population of some 5000 persons added greatly to the existing difficulties, and for a fortnight before Kut fell horse and mule flesh, and a four-ounce ration of flour, was what the garrison lived on. When the food problem became serious, numerous efforts to render help from without were made by the relieving force ; about eight tons of supplies and other stores were dropped from aeroplanes from 11th April onwards, and a heroic attempt to run a food ship through the blockade all but succeeded. The vessel selected for this purpose was the *Julnar*, one of the river steamers belonging to Lynch Brothers. She started on the night of 24th April and tried, with three hundred tons of provisions aboard, to run the gauntlet of the enemy's guns on both banks of the river for several miles. She got up as far as Magasis, but was there held up by a submerged cable stretched across the stream. The two officers in charge of her were Lieutenant-Commanders Cowley, R.N.V.R., and Firman, R.N., the former being a well-known skipper in the service of Lynch Brothers. Lieutenant-Commander Firman was killed outright, and Lieutenant-Commander

Cowley, who was slightly wounded in three places, was said to have died of his wounds, but there is strong evidence to prove that he was murdered. Both these officers were awarded the Victoria Cross. On 26th April General Townshend sent out letters to open negotiations with the Turks, and on 29th April the formal surrender took place. It was entirely due to want of food, and the Turks themselves admitted that they could never have succeeded in taking Kut by any means other than starvation. Before the garrison marched out all guns, rifles, and war materials were destroyed, but nearly 2900 British troops, about 7190 Indian troops and over 3200 followers fell into Turkish hands. Amongst them were 1075 sick and wounded, who were exchanged for an equal number of prisoners taken by us.

It is now proposed briefly to survey, in the light of subsequent events, the situation in Mesopotamia at the time of the occupation of Kut-al-Amarah by General Townshend. The British merchants, who at that time were still shut up in Baghdad, state that after the British occupation of Kut it was confidently believed in Baghdad that an immediate advance on that city would take place. So strong was this belief that the German and Austrian consuls had made all arrangements to hand over the interests of their respective Governments to the American consul, and horses and carriages were purchased by them and by the merchants and bank managers in anticipation of a hurried departure. The German doctor, who was at that time attending the few British civilians remaining in Baghdad, even came to them with the proposal that, in consideration for their undertaking to look after one or two German ladies who were unable to leave, they should be allowed to remain unmolested in the city. At the same time the doctor informed them that no opposition to the British advance was possible, as the Turkish army under Nur-ed-Din Pasha had left the river after being routed, and at that moment was scattered about the desert in great confusion. For three days Nur-ed-Din Pasha lost touch with the enemy and with Baghdad. That the British should remain passive at Kut under such circumstances was naturally incomprehensible to the inhabitants of Baghdad. The governor of the city, Sulaiman Nazif Bey, made all the necessary dispositions for evacuation, and for the maintenance of order pending the arrival of the British. The steamers *Baghdad* and *Busra* were dismantled and partially filled with materials with a view to sinking them.

At this time there was considerable friction between the Turks and the Germans, which rendered any concerted plan of action difficult. The German Military Mission under Major Klein had earned for itself the reputation of a set of sots and evil-livers, and the Turkish and German civil administrations were also at daggers drawn. Under these circumstances the British merchants declare that a strong flying column would have been sufficient to have caused an immediate exodus of the Turks and Germans. There were, moreover, vast accumulations of stores in Baghdad which could not have been removed in time.

The sequel is well known. Time passed while the Germans scoffed and the expectant population of Baghdad lost faith. Von der Goltz Pasha's staff arrived, and a new period of activity and reorganisation set in. On 6th October 1915 the

British merchants were taken away from Baghdad, and on their way up to Mosul they passed Turkish reinforcements, whom the merchants estimated at between twenty and thirty thousand, being hurried down to Ctesiphon, where they arrived in time to turn the scale against us. It is interesting to note that in the middle of October—that is to say, just at this critical juncture—the Indian Government telegraphed home to say that " the chances of eventual successful advance will not be prejudiced by delay." On 17th November the War Office telegraphed to General Nixon to say that 30,000 Turks were marching from Anatolia to Irak. These troops turned out to be the 18th Army Corps, of which the advanced parties began to arrive in Baghdad about the middle of October.

From the foregoing facts it will be seen that if General Townshend had resumed his advance immediately after the battle of Kut, he could have marched straight into Baghdad without further serious fighting and could have established himself there before Von der Goltz had time to reach that city. After the latter arrived, however, it is doubtful whether General Townshend could have remained there for a single day, and the tragedy of surrender would have been enacted in Baghdad instead of Kut. With the necessary reinforcements and means of transport General Townshend would no doubt have gone on at once ; without them the only course was not to advance at all.

CHAPTER XII

A PERSIAN CITY DURING THE GREAT WAR

The dogs bark, but the caravan passes on.—*Old Proverb.*

IN western Persia in the autumn of 1914 the most noticeable signs of the Great War were the gradual rise in prices, the irregularity of the mails, and the exodus of Germans from Persia *via* Baghdad instead of the usual Caspian Sea route. Since the Kalhurs and Galkhanis were at that time exacting heavy blackmail from all caravans and travellers on the Kermanshah-Qasr-i-Shirin road, most of these Germans had an adventurous time. Two from Teheran were kept in chains for several days at Sar-i-Pul, severely beaten, and forced to pay eighty tomans.

The first German political agents to arrive in Kermanshah were Schunemann and his assistant, Paschan. They established themselves there early in 1915. The former came ostensibly as German consul. He had been in Persia for years, at first in Azerbaijan with the Lepsius Mission, which conducted schools and orphanages for Syrians and Armenians. He was a carpenter by trade, but shrewd and well fitted for the difficult task assigned to him. At first the representatives of the Allies, which included the British and Russian consuls and a Russian captain in charge of several hundred Persian Cossacks, did not regard the presence of Schunemann as a menace, but they soon became aware that these Germans were spending money lavishly and had gathered round them a formidable body of armed retainers. They maintained their own bodyguard, and paid large sums to influential men simply to remain neutral in case of trouble.

They also bought at high prices from the tribal chiefs guarantees to furnish certain numbers of men, both horse and foot, when called upon. These pioneers of German propaganda were quickly followed by others of the same mould, most of whom travelled with consular passports. They visited all the gendarme posts and got into close touch with the Swedish and Persian officers. Some pretended to be engaged in scientific pursuits, and one, who afterwards became prominent in southern Persia, was making a collection of insects. An important item on their programme was the circulation of cleverly prepared literature.

Early in the spring of 1915 Husain Raouf Bey, with a force of about two thousand, partly regulars belonging to the 37th Division and the remainder Jof and other Kurdish tribesmen, crossed the Persian frontier and came up as far as Kerind. The people of the district protested against this advance, and some of the chiefs, including Ali Akbar Khan of the Sinjabi tribe, telegraphed to Teheran for permission to drive the Turks out. The Government, however, paid no attention, and so the Allied representatives left Kermanshah about the middle of April and went to Hamadan, which gave Schunemann and his clique complete control of the district. The Turks had not been long in Kerind before the people of that neighbourhood, angered by wanton acts of violence on the part of the soldiers, attacked the camp. Ali Akbar Khan rode from Kermanshah to Kerind in one day to take part in the fight. Many Turks were killed, but Husain Raouf Bey with his guns drove off the attackers and looted the village. As this was not down on the programme at all, Schunemann went to Kerind and persuaded the Turks to go back to Mesopotamia. In spite of this episode, the Germans pushed their preparations as rapidly as prudence would permit. They brought in quantities of arms and ammunition. Officers arrived, and began to drill the native levies. The gendarme officers, both Swedish and Persian, openly affirmed their allegiance to Germany, and thousands of Kurds, Lurs, and Persians were soon in German employ and in process of being trained *to fight Russia.* It is curious to note that the hostility of the Swedish officers of the gendarmerie to the Allies was not realised in India for some time.

In the summer of 1915 the British and Russian consuls attempted to return to Kermanshah. Accompanied by a few Cossacks and their own personal Persian retainers, they got as far as Kangavar; but Schunemann arrived at Sahneh about the same time with a force of several hundred Lurs, and refused to allow them to proceed. After a delay of more than a fortnight, and much fruitless negotiation for a suitable Persian escort, the consular party was attacked. The Persian guard holding the village did not show much fight, and Schunemann was soon master of the situation. The consuls returned to Hamadan, and the Germans to Kermanshah. This little affair gave Schunemann great prestige and did more to link the people of the district with Germany than any vaunted victory on the Western Front could have done.

Matters came to a climax about the end of November. The gendarmes confiscated the British banks in Hamadan, Sultanabad, and elsewhere, and the Allied representatives in those places had to flee. The Russians had troops in Kazvin, which town, together with others in northern Persia, they had garrisoned before the war. They at once despatched a force to Hamadan and sent movable columns to Kum and Isfahan. The design at Kum was to capture the German propagandists fleeing from Teheran, but the refugees were too quick for the Russians. The Isfahan column was intended to stop German intrigue in those parts, and apparently succeeded. The Germans, with their gendarmes and levies, met the Russians near Aveh, and were severely handled, whereupon they evacuated Hamadan, while the Russians crossed over the mountains to Asadabad.

In January 1916 the Germans brought up about 2000 Turkish troops to the Bidsurkh Pass, some five miles east of Sahneh, with a view to checking the Russian advance. This time the Turks gave guarantees of good behaviour to the Kerind people, who in return gave them safe conduct. The tribes were now so entangled in the German net and so afraid of the Russian Cossacks that they welcomed the assistance of the Turks in the inevitable struggle.

This force was what Von der Goltz Pasha had designated the " Baghdad Group," and was composed partly of the remnants of the 37th Division and partly of irregulars.

In mid-January 1916 they attacked the Russian

advance guard, which consisted of about 350
Cossacks and infantry, and compelled them to
evacuate Kangavar and retire to Asadabad.   These
were the first Turkish troops to encounter the
Russians in Persia.

For the first six weeks of 1916 life in Kermanshah was full of excitement, and murders and
highway robberies occurred constantly in open daylight.   The province was controlled by Nizam-es-
Sultaneh, a former governor of Luristan and now
the principal tool of the Germans, who sat at the
head of a sort of mock parliament in the city.
On the 22nd February, however, there was a rude
awakening ; for on the 20th the Russian 1st
Caucasus Cavalry Division, supported by the
greater part of two battalions of infantry, had
advanced from Asadabad.   On the 21st they took
the Bidsurkh Pass, and most of the Germans left
Kermanshah the following day.   The city was
panic-stricken.   The Swedes and Germans had
everywhere circulated tales of Russian cruelty
and violence, and for two days the Baghdad road
was black with people moving down towards
Mesopotamia.   The last of the Germans and
Swedes arrived from the front on the afternoon of
the 23rd.   They had very little transport, and were
therefore obliged to leave behind most of the stores
collected at Kermanshah during a whole year.
They had quantities of rifles and ammunition in
their headquarters, and one of their number was
told off to stay behind and blow up everything.
They were still struggling with their personal
belongings, and trying to load them on the few
animals at their disposal, when the sound of the
Russian artillery was heard from Kara Su bridge.
This was soon accompanied by rifle fire, and the

Germans and Swedes mounted and rode off without waiting to destroy anything. As the sun was setting, the remnant of Turks entered the town. They were only a few hundred strong, and were haggard, hungry, and dropping with fatigue. The Russians had been pounding them all the way from Sahneh. They went into the Government House, planted a gun on the roof, and refused to go any further that night. The Russians spent the night at the Kara Su, and sent in a message demanding that a deputation under a white flag meet them early in the morning and surrender the city. There was much running to and fro, and the next morning, while it was still dark, a humble procession marched out to the Kara Su, bowed to the ground before the Russian Cossacks nodding haughtily on their horses, and surrendered the city ; at ten o'clock on the 24th February 1916 the Russians entered. Kermanshah remained in their hands for the next four months. This force, which numbered about 4000, consisted principally of cavalry, and included one or two crack regiments " resting " from other fronts.

The Cossacks followed up the Turks and Germans as far as Kerind, but did not attempt for some time to advance any further. If they had continued their pursuit and had made a demonstration towards Baghdad, it might have changed the whole situation at Kut, as the Turks would have been obliged to detach an appreciable force to prevent them from joining hands with the British. The reason for their delay at this critical period is difficult to understand, the more so because at that time the ration strength of the Russians in this theatre exceeded 40,000. The Russian excuse for not advancing was the rainy weather and their

lack of transport.   In the meantime the Baghdad
Group withdrew from Persia and rejoined the
Sixth Army, which was still investing Kut.

In May, when Kut had fallen and the weather
was getting hot, the Russians advanced towards
Khanaqin.   They were without helmets, and
many of them were still in winter clothing.   The
Cossacks rode round Khanaqin, cut the Turkish
communications, captured a few convoys, sabred
some Turks, and had them photographed ; but the
attack on Khanaqin itself was a failure.   The
Russian artillery was now inferior to that of the
Turks, and the Russians had to retire.   The
Turks, having taken Kut, were now able to
detach a large force to operate against the Russians ;
and the 13th Army Corps, consisting of the 2nd,
6th, and a composite division, together with an
independent cavalry brigade—all weak units,—
was sent into Persia to pursue them.   This corps
suffered considerable casualties on the way up to
Kermanshah.   The Russians made a good withdrawal and left practically nothing of value for
their enemies.   The Turks entered Kermanshah
on the 1st July.   There was an engagement last-
ing several hours on the hills to the south-east of
the city.   The Russians fell back stubbornly across
the Kara Su, and the Turks, in attempting to follow
them up, were repulsed.   The Russians then established themselves about sixteen miles east of
Kermanshah.   The Turks entrenched opposite
them, and then rested during the fasting month of
Ramazan.

At the beginning of August, when the Turks
were preparing to advance, the ammunition dump
at their headquarters in Kermanshah took fire,
and many camels, mules and donkeys, and several

persons, were blown to pieces. The sound of the bursting shells made the townsfolk think that the Russians were bombarding the town again, and the Germans, who had opened a bank and a supply depot, turned over their money and were on the point of leaving when they found out what had happened. Driving the Russians before them, the Turks marched to Hamadan in six days, arriving there on the 11th August 1916. As a result of this fighting about 200 Turkish wounded were brought back to Kermanshah. The troops quartered in Hamadan consisted of the 2nd Division (1st, 5th, and 6th Regiments), the 6th Division (16th, 17th, and 18th Regiments) and the 44th Regiment. The people of the city were pleased when they came in, but still more pleased when they went out.

The Turks now had a great many sick. All sorts of diseases were rife among them, especially cholera, typhus, and malaria. They had eleven hospitals in Kermanshah, with an average of 2000 sick in them all the time. There were only five doctors to look after these hospitals, and there were practically no medicines. The equipment in the surgical hospital was marked " British Red Cross," and was captured in Kut. During the nine months of the Turkish occupation there was probably never a day without some deaths, and the mortality once rose to thirty a day. The Turkish commander, Ali Ihsan Bey, published an order threatening to hang all the doctors if the record did not improve. When the Turks left Kermanshah their cemetery contained at least 2500 dead. In addition to the Anatolian Turks, who were of course the backbone of the Turkish force in Persia, there were Arabs, Jews, and a few Armenians.

There were also about 600 Algerian and Moroccan Arabs captured from the French by the Germans at the beginning of the war. None of these nationalities succumbed to disease as did the Anatolian Turk.

The Turks had not been in Kermanshah long before the Germans again arrived on the scene. Nizam-es-Sultaneh and his cabinet also came back and re-established themselves there. The Germans tried to reorganise the gendarmerie and the battalions of levies, but the people were more wary. They were willing to take German money, but they flatly refused to fight. They were afraid of being drafted into the Turkish army, and since the action at Aveh they had a wholesome dread of Russian shrapnel and Russian Cossacks. It was remarkable how the Persian regiments would melt away when the Germans tried to put them into any position that seemed at all dangerous. The Germans became very disheartened, and some of them did not hesitate to say that their mission was a failure. Early in 1917 there were persistent rumours of an impending British advance in Mesopotamia, but the first definite indication in Kermanshah of the march of events in that region was the hurried evacuation of the Turkish hospitals. It took a fortnight to get away the sick and to remove the grain and other essential supplies the Turks had collected in that city. They had practically no transport of their own, so they commandeered thousands of donkeys from the inhabitants. If a man were too ill to ride a donkey by himself he was held on by soldiers walking on each side of it. Men and animals died like flies all along the road.

On the morning of the 9th March the sound of

Russian guns was again heard on the Hamadan road, and by noon they were firing from the Kara Su bridge. That afternoon the Turkish main body withdrew into Kermanshah, having previously blown up one of the arches of the bridge, and the guns of their rear-guard shelled the Russians all that afternoon and throughout the next day. Late in the afternoon of the 10th the Russians crossed the river by a ford, but were thrown back. The Turkish army evacuated the city during the night, and on the morning of the 11th March their rear-guard, still shelling the Russians, was seen disappearing over the hills.

Once more Kermanshah was under the Russians. They pursued the Turks as far as Pa-i-Tak, where Ali Ihsan Bey held them up for more than a week till his preparations for crossing the Sirivan River were complete. When the weather grew hot, the Russians evacuated Qasr-i-Shirin and the adjacent country, but they retained a garrison at Kerind through the summer until their animals had eaten or destroyed the harvest. The effect of the revolution was already very noticeable in the discipline of their troops. Officers were disobeyed and even threatened, and the men did as they pleased.

The Russians had a great deal of trouble with the Kurds. The tribes were at first willing to make friends, but the now undisciplined soldiers committed various acts of violence and roused the anger of the Kurds. The Galkhani tribe was especially active, and Russian convoys were attacked and camps raided constantly. The Russians in retaliation looted various villages along the road, Kerind itself suffering severely. In August a meeting was held with the tribal chiefs and a truce was arranged, but both parties were distrustful, and when the Russians went to Mesopotamia in the autumn to join the British they avoided the main road and marched by way of Gilan.

From time to time all through the summer and autumn parties of Russians left for home, but they were still in evidence in the beginning of 1918 when General Dunsterville's force began to arrive. They evacuated the city soon afterwards, and for the next three years Kermanshah enjoyed the blessings of British occupation.   Fields were culti-vated that had not been touched for years ; travellers came and went without fear of molesta-tion or blackmail ; and once more the old road rang with the music of caravans.

From this brief record of events it will be seen that within a space of three years the quaint old Persian city of Kermanshah was occupied twice by the Turks and Germans, twice by the Russians, and once by the British, which, considering that Persia was a neutral country, affords a striking indication of how widespread and continuous was the havoc wrought by the Great War.

TEHERAN,
November 1920.

CHAPTER XIII

THE TURKISH ARMY IN THE GREAT WAR

In this chapter it is proposed to set down certain facts and figures regarding the Turkish Army and to explain some of its more obscure formations. Orders of battle at several decisive stages of the war have been added, by way of further elucidating the part played by Turkey in the great struggle.

A complete order of battle of the whole Turkish Army is unfortunately too lengthy a statement to be included, as it deals with no less than 63 regular infantry divisions and 7 Caucasus infantry divisions, or 70 in all ; also with 191 regular regiments and 17 Caucasus regiments. Of the 70 divisions some 25 regular and all the Caucasus divisions were formed after the outbreak of war.

The records in the Ministry of War at Constantinople show that in August 1914 the Turkish Army consisted of 38 infantry divisions—namely, those numbered from 1 to 40—excluding the 19th and 20th, which were not formed till the beginning of 1915. Very few of these divisions were up to peace strength, and there were not more than 150,000 combatants in the whole Turkish Army. From the date of the order for general mobilisation up to the signing of the

Armistice, nearly 2,700,000 men were called to arms, making a grand total of 2,850,000 men.   When it is considered that the number of adult males in the Ottoman Empire, including Arabs, Circassians, Kurds, Moslem immigrants from many lands, Armenians, Jews, Greeks, and others, who were eligible for military service when war was declared, or who became eligible during the four succeeding years, was perhaps less than four and a half millions, it will be admitted that these Turkish mobilisation figures represent a great achievement. The strength of the Turkish Army appears to have reached its maximum about May 1916—that is to say, just after the fall of Kut-al-Amarah, —when it comprised 43 divisions and aggregated roughly 650,000 combatants.   The Turkish General Staff estimates their total casualties, up to the signing of the Armistice, at nearly two millions, including deserters.   This is of course merely an estimate, and perhaps rather a high one ;   the organisation necessary for an accurate record of casualties did not exist in the Turkish Army. The number of deserters was undoubtedly very large, and is supposed to have reached the amazing total of 400,000.

During this war the Turkish Army has contained several formations and units which have puzzled us considerably.   A description of some of these may therefore be of interest.

The Yildirim Army Group.—*Yildirim* means lightning ; it was applied as a nickname to Sultan Bayazid at the end of the fourteenth century, and alluded to the rapidity of his movements.

The Yildirim Army Group was formed on 15th July 1917, with the object of recapturing Baghdad, and was to consist of the Sixth Army, already in

Mesopotamia, and the Seventh Army, which was being newly formed in Constantinople from the troops returning from Galicia, Rumania, and Macedonia. The original scheme was, however, practically strangled at birth.

For strategical reasons the Palestine front, which was then being held by the Fourth Army, was taken over by the Eighth Army, the Fourth Army Command being changed to that of " The Syrian and Western Arabian General Command," with its headquarters at Damascus. This change did not last long, and on 17th January 1918 it again became that of the Fourth Army and was placed under the Yildirim Army Group, the 48th Division, the Amman Expeditionary Force, and some scattered units being added on 23rd February. The Sixth Army was no longer shown as belonging to the Yildirim, which now, therefore, consisted of the Fourth, Seventh, and Eighth Armies. Marshal Liman von Sanders was appointed to the Yildirim Command in February 1918, in place of Marshal von Falkenhayn, but he did not actually take over the command till 1st March. After the Palestine retreat the Eighth Army headquarters were disbanded at Smyrna on 10th October. Those of the Fourth Army were disbanded on 15th October, and those of the Seventh and Yildirim Army Group itself on 4th November. At the time of the retreat the Second Army was also placed under the Yildirim. Its headquarters were disbanded on 15th December.

The following is a translation of the original order for the formation of the Yildirim Army Group :—

" GENERAL HEADQUARTERS,
" 15th September 1917.

" 1. A new group command will be formed under the name of the Yildirim Army Group Command. The group commander will remain in Constantinople for the present.

" 2. Field-Marshal von Falkenhayn Pasha has been appointed commander of the Yildirim Army Group, and Colonel von Dummes Bey has been appointed chief of his staff.

" 3. The Sixth and Seventh Armies will come under the Yildirim Army Group.

" 4. For the present the Order of Battle will be as follows :—

" (a) Sixth Army.—13th Army Corps. 2nd, 6th, and 14th Divisions.
18th Army Corps. 14th, 51st, and 52nd Divisions.
" (b) Seventh Army.—3rd Army Corps. 24th, 50th, and 59th Divisions.
15th Army Corps. 19th and 20th Divisions.
" (c) German Asiatic Column.

" 5. The Sixth Army Group will be placed under the command of the Yildirim Army Group from the 16th September 1917.

" 6. The headquarter personnel of the Seventh Army will be completed by the Ministry of War as soon as possible. When this has been done, the Seventh Army will come under the command of the Yildirim Army Group.

" 7. For the present the headquarters of the Seventh Army will be in Constantinople. The troops of the Seventh Army will be placed under the command of that Army as soon as they reach

Constantinople. The First Army in Constantinople will keep the Seventh Army Command informed as to the arrival of these troops.

" 8. The instructions regarding the official relationship between the Army Commands and the Yildirim Army Group Command will be issued as a separate order.

" 9. The Second and Fourth Armies and the Yildirim Army Group will exchange daily war reports.

" 10. The telegraphic address of the Yildirim Army Group headquarters will be ' Yildirim Group Command, Constantinople.'

" 11. This address will be sent to all telegraphic centres in the Empire by the Yildirim Army Group Command, who will be responsible that this order is carried out.

" (Signed) ENVER,

" Vice-Generalissimo.

"No. 5392."

Mevlevi Battalions.—At the outbreak of war the Mevlevi, or Dancing Dervish, community offered their services to the Empire in order to encourage recruiting and to give religious support to the Army. It will be recalled that these Mevlevis have monasteries in various parts of the Ottoman Empire, and have considerable influence amongst certain classes of the people. The offer was accepted, and a battalion 800 strong, consisting entirely of Mevlevi dervishes, was formed in December 1914, at Konia, the Mevlevi capital. From there it was sent down to Damascus, where it remained for two years. At the end of August 1916 a second battalion was added, and the two battalions formed into the Mevlevi Regiment. The 2nd battalion was not composed of dervishes, but of ordinary recruits. The regiment did no fighting until the final phases of the Palestine operations, and was disbanded at the end of September 1918.

The Constantinople Fire Brigade.—A famous regiment forming part of the First Army. Their permanent station is Constantinople, and their principal duties, in addition to military training as a fighting unit, are those of an ordinary city fire brigade, but they also furnish guards at places like the Ministry of War, and they attend ceremonial parades, such as the *Selamlik*, in which they take a picturesque part. They are popularly known as the Constantinople Fire Brigade, or Sapeurs Pompiers, but their real name is the *Itfaiye Alai*, or Fire-Extinguishing Regiment.

Their pre-war establishment was four battalions, composed of men specially selected from line regiments. They had no machine-guns. During the war five additional battalions were raised, making nine in all. The 2nd and 4th Battalions were sent to Mesopotamia, and two new ones, the 5th and 6th, and a company, were raised in Constantinople to take their places. Shortly afterwards this company was expanded into the 7th Battalion. The 1st, 3rd, 5th, and 6th Battalions were sent to Gallipoli to join the Fifth Army. An eighth battalion, formed from a nucleus taken out of the 7th, was raised in 1917 ; and on 13th July 1918 a ninth battalion was added. At the beginning of 1919 only three battalions existed, namely, the 7th, 8th, and 9th.

The Osmanjik Battalion.—At the beginning of the war about 450 Fidais were collected together under Lieutenant-Colonel Sulaiman Askeri Bey, and formed into what was termed the Osmanjik

Battalion. They were originally intended to be sent on special service to the Russian shores of the Black Sea, but that scheme was abandoned and they were sent to Mesopotamia instead. There this curious formation was further obscured by being amalgamated with the remnants of the 1st/26th Regiment and renamed the 1st Muretteb Battalion. The Fidais did not constitute an official Turkish organisation.

Muretteb Units.—The term *muretteb*, which came into general use in the Balkan War of 1912, is applied to any temporary or composite formation not larger than a regiment. There were many *muretteb* units in the Turkish Army during the Great War, but nowadays the term is not used in respect of a division, arbitrary formations of this size or larger being known either as groups, field detachments, or expeditionary forces as the case may be.

Depot Formations.—These were formed with a view to keeping units up to their full strength. The original scheme was to provide each regiment with a depot battalion, and each division with a depot regiment. However, towards the end of 1917 the supply of reinforcements for the field armies began to fall seriously short of the demand, and depot regiments themselves were sent into the line and used as regular units. As these were gradually destroyed, new depot regiments were formed at selected centres in the area of each army. No depot divisions were formed. Towards the end of the war these depot formations were organised as a separate command under an Inspector, who was a Major-General.

Non-Commissioned Officers' Training Units.— After the general mobilisation it was found that the Non-Commissioned Officers' Training School was inadequate to furnish anything like the number of N.C.O.'s required by the Army. In order to supplement the supply, several training units were formed in Constantinople, in which the N.C.O.'s of each arm and branch of the service were trained separately.

Muhafiz Units.—Troops used independently for local protection. Sometimes they consisted of the whole, or part, of a regular infantry or cavalry regiment, sent to a particular centre on special duty ; sometimes, as in the case of the Constantinople Muhafiz Regiment, they contained as many as four complete battalions. During the war, Muhafiz units were occasionally posted to divisions as ordinary reinforcements. A *Sahil Muhafiz Tabur* is a coastguard battalion.

The Milli Tribe.—A Kurdish tribe of the Diarbekir Vilayet. About the time of the Constitution Ibrahim Pasha rebelled against the Turkish Government and proclaimed the independence of his tribe. The Millis, being Kurds, are not liable to military service in times of peace, but during war they are expected to provide a certain number or irregular horse and foot. Accordingly, in December 1914, they sent a body of horsemen into the Sari Kamish area, but they returned without doing any fighting. Their next venture was to send some men, both mounted and dismounted, down to Nasiriyah, and these took part in the Turkish attempt to recapture Basrah.

There was no regular unit in the Turkish Army which was composed wholly or even partly of Millis during the war. Nevertheless, the dismounted Millis with Sulaiman Askeri became known, however incorrectly, as the Milli Battalion.

The Turkish terms *Millis,* militia, and *Gunulu,* volunteer, are used synonymously, and the fact that volunteers when taken prisoner often described themselves as *Millis,* meaning volunteers, has possibly led to confusion.

The Islam Army.—The name given to the national army of the Muhammadan peoples of the Caucasus, which was raised in 1918 under Nuri Pasha.

After the Russian revolution, both the Georgians and the Armenians began to reorganise their armies, and in doing so they received some assistance from the Germans. The Muhammadans of the Caucasus then began to do likewise, and they applied to Turkey for help. The Islam Army scheme never received the official sanction of the Turkish Cabinet, but it had the entire approval of Enver Pasha, who saw in it not only great political possibilities, but also an opportunity for providing his brother with a lucrative appointment. Service with the Islam Army was optional, but a step in promotion was given to every officer and non-commissioned officer who joined it. Altogether about 150 officers and a large number of other ranks took service under Nuri Pasha, who was also promised the loan of the 5th Caucasus Division until the venture became a going concern. The headquarters of the Islam Army were at first at Genjeh and then at Baku. After the Armistice was signed all the regular officers and other ranks who were with Nuri Pasha were recalled by the Ministry of War, but it is by no means certain that they all obeyed the summons. The special orders of battle which are given further on include one of the Islam Army.

Caucasus Formations.—After the battle of Sari

Kamish in January 1915 the Third Army, which consisted of the 9th, 10th, and 11th Army Corps, became very weak and towards the end of 1915 the 5th Army Corps was transferred from the Dardanelles and added to the Third Army.

After the fall of Erzerum in February 1916, and of Erzinjan in July 1916, the ranks of the Third Army became once more depleted, and so the army commander, Lieutenant-General Vehib Pasha, proposed to reorganise his army by forming two new Army Corps, to be known as the 1st and 2nd Caucasus Army Corps, out of the four existing ones, which were to become Caucasus divisions, the old divisions becoming Caucasus regiments. The scheme received the approval of Enver Pasha and came into force on 12th September 1916.

The Third or Caucasus Army had its headquarters at Soushehri, and as reorganised consisted of six infantry divisions and a cavalry brigade, as follows :—

Army Corps.	Division.	Regiments.
1st Caucasus	9th Caucasus	17th, 28th, and 29th Caucasus Regts.
	10th Caucasus	30th, 31st, and 32nd Caucasus Regts.
2nd Caucasus	5th Caucasus	9th, 10th, and 13th Caucasus Regts.
	11th Caucasus	18th, 33rd, and 34th Caucasus Regts.
	Independent Divisions.	
	36th Caucasus	106th, 107th, 108th Regiments.
	37th Caucasus	109th, 110th, 111th Regiments.
Cavalry	2nd Cavalry Brigade	

The only Caucasus division not included in the above is the 3rd, which was formed in March 1918, and sent to the Ninth Army. When, however, the reader studies the order of battle for the Islam Army he will find that mention is there made of the 1st, 2nd, and 4th Caucasus divisions. These have not been inserted in the above list for the following reasons :—The Islam Army was formed from non-Ottoman Muhammadans, and although it was never a part of the Turkish Regular Army it was organised on similar lines. The divisions composing it were all given the name of Caucasus divisions, although only one of them, the 5th, which perhaps never actually joined the Islam Army, was a regular unit. The other three, namely, the 1st, 2nd, and 4th, were not really Caucasus divisions at all, within the accepted meaning of the term, and corresponded roughly to the Imperial Service Troops of the Indian Army.

Thus the seven Caucasus divisions proper were 3rd, 5th, 9th, 10th, 11th, 36th, and 37th ; and the seventeen Caucasus regiments proper were 7th to 11th (inclusive), 13th, 17th, 18th, and 28th to 37th (inclusive). The three Caucasus divisions of the Islam Army were 1st, 2nd, and 4th. The eight Caucasus regiments of the Islam Army were 1st to 6th (inclusive), 12th, and 14th.

Expeditionary Forces and Groups.—The Turks refer to an expeditionary force as a *Kouveh Seferiye,* and to a field detachment as a *Mufrezeh.* From the following list, which contains some of the principal of them, it will be seen that many formations of this type were organised by the Turks during the Great War.

1st Expeditionary Force.—Formed shortly after the general mobilisation from the 7th, 8th, and 9th Regiments of the 3rd Division, and sent to the Caucasus and Persia at the end of 1914.

Canal Expeditionary Force.—Formed at the end of 1914 from part of the 10th Division. After the attack on the Suez Canal these troops were sent back to the Dardanelles, the 3rd Division, with some guns and cavalry, taking their places.

Hejaz Expeditionary Force.—At the outbreak of war this consisted of the 22nd (Independent) Division. In addition to furnishing the garrisons of Mecca, Medina, and Taif, it was strung out along the Hejaz railway in the neighbourhood of Medina, but after the middle of 1915 it was withdrawn into the city itself. The bulk of this force was captured at the end of 1916, when its place was taken by the 58th Division. This latter consisted of the 42nd, 55th, and 162nd Regiments, the 58th Artillery Regiment, an Engineer company, about 30 machine-guns, and no cavalry. The artillery consisted of two field and two mountain batteries. This division, under the command of Major-General Fakhriddin Pasha, was the last unit of the Turkish Army to surrender, and then only did so in January 1919 by special command of the Sultan of Turkey.

5th Expeditionary Force.—Formed at the end of 1914 by taking a regiment from each of the three divisions of the 5th Army Corps. It was sent at first to the south-east of Van, and then to Selmas to protect the right flank of the Third Army retreating from Sari Kamish. This force eventually became the 52nd Division.

Turkey-in-Europe Force.—This force, known to the Turks and Germans as the Rumeli Field Detachment, was formed towards the end of 1915 from the 177th Regiment, with two mountain guns and a squadron of cavalry, and was sent to Monastir early in 1916. At the beginning of 1918 the 177th Regiment was transferred to the Ninth Army, whereupon the Turkey-in-Europe Force ceased to exist.

The Amman Expeditionary Force.—In March 1918, when Marshal Liman von Sanders took over the command of the Palestine forces from Marshal von Falkenhayn, the 20th Army Corps was operating to the east of the Jordan. It was immediately sent across the river to hold up the attack towards Nablus. After this a small force called the Jordan Group was sent to the east of the Jordan, the group being subsequently reinforced by a part of the 48th Division. The Turkish front, from the east of the Jordan right down to Medina, was known as the Fourth Army front. With the object of holding Ma'an against the attacks of the Sherifial forces, all the troops along the Hejaz railway south of Dera'a were concentrated at Ma'an and designated the Ma'an Expeditionary Force. This title was soon changed to that of the Amman Expeditionary Force, which shortly afterwards, by a special order of the Yildirim Army Group, was turned into the 62nd Division.

Mosul Group.—Formed in July 1916 from the 10th and 11th Regiments of the 4th Division, with the object of protecting Mosul from attack by the Russians. The Mosul Group was partly destroyed and partly captured in September 1916.

Euphrates Group.—An independent force, operating on the Euphrates under the direct orders of the Sixth Army commander. This arrangement was made because of the great difficulties of communication between the forces on the Euphrates and those on the Tigris. At first it consisted of the 156th Regiment, which was captured early in 1917. The 50th Division then formed the

Euphrates Group, but was captured in March 1918, its place being taken by the 5th Division, to which was attached the 24th Regiment and a composite cavalry regiment.

Tigris Group.—After the fall of Baghdad the 14th Division became designated the Tigris Group. It was captured on 28th March 1918. There was also the "Baghdad Group," which is referred to in Chapter XII.

Dates of the Formation and Disbandment of the nine Turkish Armies

No.	Date of Formation.	Date of first Disband- ment.	Re-formed.	Finally Disbanded.
1st Army	5/8/14	17/2/18	24/9/18	11/10/18
2nd Army	5/8/14	18/11/14	5/12/14	15/12/18
3rd Army	5/8/14	—	—	15/11/18
4th Army	7/9/14	26/9/17	19/1/18	15/10/18
5th Army	25/3/15	—	—	21/11/18
6th Army	5/9/15	Still in existence in January 1919.		
7th Army	11/8/17	—	—	13/11/18
8th Army	2/10/17	—	—	14/11/18
9th Army	9/6/18	Still in existence in January 1919.		

It is now proposed to give the Turkish orders of battle at certain decisive stages of the war. It must be borne in mind that the information in the following pages is drawn entirely from Turkish sources, and that it does not in every case tally with our own. The compositions of the Islam Army and the Ninth Army have also been added. The orders of battle in Gallipoli have been given in Chapter X.

1. Battle of Sari Kamish

The strength and formation of the Third Turkish Army during the Sari Kamish fighting (*i.e.* from 26th December 1914 to 5th January 1915) were as follows :—

9th Army Corps.—17th, 28th, and 29th Divisions.

At the time of the crossing of the Russo-Turkish frontier (*i.e.* 24th December 1914) this Army Corps, with its three divisions, comprised 18,000 combatants, but by the end of December 1914, owing to the Bardiz and Sari Kamish fighting and the severity of the winter, the whole Army Corps had been reduced to 1000 infantry, 40 mountain-guns (of which one-half were damaged), and 16 machine-guns.

10th Army Corps.—30th, 31st, and 32nd Divisions.

Arrived in the Sari Kamish area on 29th December 1914. On 30th December 1914 the combatant strength of the 30th and 31st Divisions was reduced to 1800 infantry, eight Q.F. field-guns, 16 Q.F. mountain-guns, and no machine-guns. The 32nd Division was located partially at Bardiz and partially to the north of Yeni Keui. By the end of December the division had been reduced to 500 infantry, eight mountain-guns and three machine-guns.

11th Army Corps.—18th, 33rd, and 34th Divisions.

On 3rd January 1915 this Army Corps was on the Medjingert - Altoun Bulak - Kelek line. On 6th January 1915 the strength of the whole Army Corps was so reduced that it was found impossible to form a division out of the remnants of its three divisions.

13th Army Corps.—37th Division.

Took part in the operations along the Malazgert-Totak line.

Two regular cavalry divisions, viz. the 2nd Regular Division and the 1st Mixed Division, consisting of the 1st Lancers and the 5th Regular Cavalry, also took part in the Sari Kamish fighting. Their total strength was about 6000 sabres.

On 2nd January 1915 the 9th and 10th Army Corps were combined under the name of the Left Flank Army.

2. FALL OF ERZERUM

On 13th February 1916, the Russians commenced to attack Erzerum, and on 16th February 1916 they occupied the town. In this battle the composition of the Third Turkish Army was as follows :—

9th Army Corps.—17th and 28th Divisions.
10th Army Corps.—31st, 32nd, and 34th Divisions.
11th Army Corps.—18th, 29th, and 33rd Divisions.

Two Cavalry Divisions.

The combatant strength of the 9th Army Corps was 313 officers and 7864 men. That of the 10th and 11th Army Corps was less in both cases.

3. CAPTURE OF KUT-AL-AMARAH

The strength and the formation of the Sixth Turkish Army on the date of the capture of the town (29th April 1916) were as follows :—

13th Army Corps.—2nd and 35th Divisions; one Independent Cavalry Brigade. Located to the east of Kut-al-Amarah.

18th Army Corps.—45th Division, round Kut-al-Amarah ; 51st and 52nd Divisions, east of Kut-al-Amarah.

6th Division.—Was under the orders of the Sixth Army, and was partially engaged in the firing-line against the relief force east of Kut-al-Amarah.

Baghdad Group.—Was withdrawn from Persia to Khanaqin on account of the pressure of the Russians.

The total combatant strength of the Sixth Army was then 35,313 of all ranks.

4. FALL OF ERZINJAN

On 1–2nd July 1916 the Russians commenced to attack with much superior forces, and on 24th July 1916 Erzinjan was evacuated for strategical reasons. The Second and Third Turkish Armies took part in this fighting.

Formation and Strength of the Second Army :—

2nd Army Corps.—11th and 12th Divisions.
3rd Army Corps.—1st, 7th, and 14th Divisions.
4th Army Corps.—47th and 48th Divisions.
16th Army Corps.—5th and 8th Divisions.
The total combatant strength of this army was then 17,474 of all ranks.

Formation and Strength of the Third Army :—

5th Army Corps.—9th, 10th, and 13th Divisions.
9th Army Corps.—17th and 29th Divisions.
10th Army Corps.—30th, 31st, and 32nd Divisions.
Kemakh Group.—28th and 36th Divisions.
Two Cavalry Divisions.
The total combatant strength of this army was then 27,231 of all ranks.

5. FALL OF BAGHDAD

Baghdad fell on 11th March 1917. The formation and strength of the Sixth Turkish Army at that time were as follows :—

13th Army Corps.—2nd and 6th Divisions and one Independent Cavalry Brigade. This Army Corps was retiring from Persia, with its advance guard at Khanaqin and its rear-guard at Mahidasht.

18th Army Corps.—14th, 51st, and 52nd Divisions in the firing-line north of Baghdad.

Euphrates and Sulimanieh Detachments.—Each consisted of a small mixed force.

The total combatant strength of this army was then 15,893 of all ranks.

6. FIRST BATTLE OF GAZA

The first Battle of Gaza took place on 26th March 1917. The formation and strength of the Fourth Turkish Army in this battle were as follows :—

22nd Army Corps.—3rd Division at Gaza ; 16th Division at Tel-esh-Sheria ; 53rd Division, the advance guard of this division was at Mezhdil.

3rd Cavalry Division at Beersheba.

The total combatant strength of this army was then 54,158 of all ranks.

7. FORMATION OF THE YILDIRIM ARMY GROUP

This group was formed on 15th July 1917, and was composed of the Sixth and Seventh Armies.

Sixth Army

13th Army Corps.—2nd Division at Penjvin ; 6th Division at Kara Tepe (south of Ḳifri) ;

46th Division at Mosul ; one Independent Cavalry Brigade at Shirvan Kale ; 14th Division at Shereemeh.

18th Army Corps.—51st and 52nd Divisions near Tikrit.

A detached portion of this army was known as the Euphrates Group.

Another detached portion appears to have retained the name of the Mosul Group after the Mosul Group proper had been destroyed.

Seventh Army

3rd Army Corps.—24th, 50th, and 59th Divisions, was in transit from Macedonia and Galicia to Constantinople and Aleppo.

15th Army Corps.—19th and 20th Divisions, as above.

German Asiatic Column.[1]—One Infantry Brigade. (Did not arrive.)

The total combatant strength of these armies was then 32,403 of all ranks.

8. Second Battle of Gaza

The second Battle of Gaza took place in November 1917. The formation and strength of the Eighth Turkish Army at that time were as follows :—

20th Army Corps.—16th Division plus a detachment at Kharabeh Abou Djerah.

22nd Army Corps.—3rd, 7th, 29th, and 54th Divisions, was strung out along the coast as far as Kharab-el-Bab.

27th Division and 3rd Cavalry Division at Beersheba.

---

[1] The German Infantry Brigade that was promised for this Asiatic Column did not arrive.

The total combatant strength of this army was then 29,118 of all ranks.

9. FALL OF JERUSALEM (9th December 1917)

The formation and strength of the troops which took part in this fighting were as follows :—

Eighth Army (Yildirim Army Group)

22nd Army Corps.—3rd, 7th, and 20th Divisions, occupying a line from the north of Jaffa up to Haifa.

Asiatic Group.—16th and 54th Divisions.

Seventh Army (Yildirim Army Group)

3rd Army Corps.—19th and 24th Divisions, north of Jerusalem.

20th Army Corps.—26th and 53rd Divisions, east of Jerusalem.

3rd Cavalry Division in El-Bura area.

Fourth Army

8th Army Corps.—43rd Division at Maalka Aliya; 48th Division at Amman—a detachment at Amman, a detachment at Tebuk; 58th Division (Hejaz Expeditionary Force) in Medina.

12th Army Corps.—23rd Division at Mersina; 41st Division between Antakia and Bilan; 44th Division at Toprak Kale.

The total combatant strength of these armies was 45,628 of all ranks.

10. FORMATION OF THE ISLAM ARMY

The Islam Army was formed on 3rd March 1918, its composition being as follows :—

1st Caucasus Infantry Division.—1st, 2nd, and 3rd Caucasus Regiments.

2nd Caucasus Infantry Division.—4th, 5th, and 6th Caucasus Regiments.

3rd Caucasus Infantry Division.—7th, 8th, and 11th Caucasus Regiments.

4th Caucasus Infantry Division.—12th and 14th Caucasus Regiments.

1st Caucasus Cavalry Division.—At first this consisted of the 2nd and 3rd Caucasus Cavalry Regiments, but on 15th September 1918 the 4th Caucasus Cavalry Regiment, which had just been formed, was added to this division.

11. FORMATION OF THE NINTH ARMY

The Ninth Army was formed on 9th June 1918. The headquarters of this army were formed from the 2nd Caucasus Army Corps headquarters.

Formation and Strength of the Ninth Army

1st Caucasus Army Corps.—10th and 11th Caucasus Divisions and 15th Division.

4th Army Corps.—5th and 36th Caucasus Divisions and 12th Division.

On 20th June 1918 the 36th Caucasus Division was transferred to the Tnird Army. The Ninth Army was thereupon re-formed as follows :—

1st Caucasus Army Corps.—5th and 12th Caucasus Divisions and 12th Division.

4th Army Corps.—9th and 10th Caucasus Divisions and 15th Division.

After the re-formation, the total combatant strength of this army was 25,354 of all ranks.

CHAPTER XIV

THE CRIMEA IN 1910

It is a remarkable thing that in these days of travel so few people should have visited the Crimea. The war of 1854–56 will always possess a peculiar attraction, not only for us, but also the French, Turks, Italians, and even the Russians themselves. The journey there by sea lies for the most part through scenery of singular beauty, and can be quickly and easily accomplished ; yet it is a rare thing to meet anyone who has visited these battle-fields. Since the Great War the peninsula has been in the throes of revolution, and the gate is still closed ; consequently a description by a modern pilgrim of some of its historical scenes may prove of interest.

The Crimean War, it will be recalled, was fought in the defence of Turkey, but although at the time of the battle of Inkerman there were about 11,000 Turkish troops in the Crimea, the soldiers of the Prophet had no opportunity of proving their worth, nearly all the fighting being done by their Christian allies.

The town of Sevastopol, which was practically destroyed during the siege, has since been entirely rebuilt. A few of the houses to which any special interest attaches, such as the private residences of

Totleben and Nakhimoff, have been restored, and their fronts adorned with explanatory mural tablets. Near the quay there is a handsome statue to Admiral Nakhimoff, the man who annihilated the Turkish fleet at Sinope. In front of General Totleben's house there now stands a military museum, full of relics, models, and pictures of the war ; and next door to it there is a memorial church. Of recent years the Russian Admiralty reserved the accommodation in the harbour for their own use. The port has therefore ceased to be a commercial one, and all its trade has been transferred to Theodosia.

Immediately the visitor lands in the Crimea his difficulties begin. He soon finds that no language is of any use to him then except Russian. There are, moreover, no guides of any kind, and no English guide-books ; and the sale of plans, and even of photographs, of the battlefields is strictly prohibited. The inscriptions on the Russian monuments are in Russian only ; they have not followed the example which we have set them in this respect. The epitaph, for instance, on Sir George Cathcart's grave, on the hill which bears his name, is in both English and Russian ; whilst the inscription on the huge obelisk, in the British Cemetery at Scutari, is in no less than four languages. But though the Russians do not cater for the comfort of visitors to the Crimea, still, strange as it may seem, they take more pride in its historical scenes than we do. So difficult was it to get along without a knowledge of Russian that I had begun to despair of seeing anything of the battlefields, when the British consul came to my aid. He drew up a programme which would take three days to get through ; and it was more than gratifying to find that the arrangements for the first day included a drive with him from Sevastopol to Balaclava and back, as the information thus gained would be invaluable to me during the rest of the time when I should be alone.   We accordingly started off up the Woronzoff road, which runs along the bottom of a deep ravine, and leads out in the direction of Cathcart's Hill.   As soon as we had arrived at a convenient bend in the road, we got out and walked up the hill to the British Cemetery, where there was a Union Jack flying. The cemetery, which was being well looked after by a German gardener, had recently been enclosed by a high stone wall.   The British Government pays £250 annually for the upkeep of it ; but the specific act which led to this additional expenditure was the theft of one of the bronze lions from the cenotaph erected by the Royal Engineers.   Having obtained a clear view of the line of the Russian defences, the Inkerman ridges, and the Valley of the Shadow of Death, we descended the hill and walked over to the ground where the charge of the Light Brigade took place.   The Russians have erected a monument on the rise where their batteries stood on the memorable 25th of October.   The work of the British cavalry at Balaclava was certainly magnificent ; but in fairness to the other arms, it must not be forgotten that practically the only other occasion on which they were engaged during the war was at the Alma, and that in getting four clasps for two days' fighting they may be said to have won their honours fairly cheaply.   Close by are the sites of the charge of the Heavy Brigade and the infantry encounter.   There is a small British monument marking the spot where our infantry were charged by the Russian cavalry, an affray

the seriousness of which is often exaggerated.
We then drove on through the village of Kadikoi
to Balaclava—the former being a small farming
centre, and the latter a popular seaside resort.

The harbour of Balaclava is almost completely
landlocked. To anyone approaching it from the
sea it is absolutely indistinguishable almost up to
the very moment of entering it. The passengers,
indeed, wonder where on earth they are going;
they seem to be charging an unbroken line of cliffs.
In the evenings Balaclava presents quite a lively
scene. There is generally a band playing, and the
cafés and promenades are thronged with people.
As there is no tide in the Black Sea, the harbour is
more like a lake than anything else, and is generally
crowded with rowing and sailing boats. On our
way back to Sevastopol we passed the house where
the brave and courteous Lord Raglan breathed his
last. It is now a well-kept private residence.

The next day was devoted to a reconnaissance
of the Russian defences round Sevastopol. This,
on foot, over rough ground, and under a July sun,
is a strenuous and thirsty undertaking. But the
only way to get a real grasp of the situation is to
walk over the actual ground. The arrangement
of the Russian trenches for the protection of the
city was quite simple, and consisted of a main line
of defence, probably nearly five miles in length,
which ran irregularly along the commanding
ridges round the inner, or man-of-war, harbour.
This line was made up of strongly fortified posts,
linked together by well-executed entrenchments,
and further strengthened by advanced works.
The Russians had recently marked out this line by
means of a low stone wall, which, though merely
outlining the works, shows the names of the units

engaged and the extent of front allotted to them.
The positions of advanced works are indicated by
monuments, whilst those of different Russian
batteries are marked by small pillars with the
numbers on them.   In view of these facts it might
reasonably be supposed that, even without any
knowledge of Russian or of the military history
of the campaign, the identification of the cardinal
points in the line of defence would be a matter of
simplicity.   But that is not altogether the case.
There are confusing elements as well.   For instance,
if you were to meet a Russian officer in the entrenchments, and you were to ask him where theMalakhoff
was situated,he would tell you that he did not know.
This reply would be a sledge-hammer blow to your
intelligence and your curiosity alike.   The explanation, however, is that whilst we apply the term to a
work, the Russians apply it to a hill ; and unless
you use the expression "Malakhoff Kurgan," he
will be just as puzzled as a Londoner would be if
a Russian said to him, "Where is the Ludgate?"
What we call the Malakhoff, the Russians call
Korniloff's Bastion ; and they know it by no other
name.   Similarly the work which the allies, and
especially the French, knew so well as the Mamelon
Vert, the Russians call the Kamchatskie Lunette.
Unless the visitor happens to know these obscure
local names, he may have some difficulty in fixing
his position.

Starting at the eastern end of the defences, there
is not much to arrest the attention of a visitor,
except perhaps the site of the little Redan, until
he comes to the Malakhoff Hill.   There he will find
a dilapidated tower of white stone, built in the
shape of a circle with a large segment cut out of it
on the town side, and with a high glacis thrown up

round it. As the visitor surveys the scene from
the top of this exposed and conspicuous bastion,
which will go down to posterity in England as the
Malakhoff, he will easily realise how it was that
some of the Russian guns came to be knocked
bodily off the tower, like bottles off a wall, by the
artillery of the allies.   Close to this tower is a bronze
statue of Korniloff, representing the famous Russian
admiral just as he had received his mortal wound ;
and in rear of it there is a French monument to
those who fell in the capture of the hill.   Facing
in the direction of Cathcart's Hill, the visitor will
notice a stony hillock, about three or four hundred
yards away to his left front, with a monument on
it consisting of a tall and slender column of bronze,
set on a granite plinth on which is written the
words " Kamchatskie Lunette."   As explained
above, this marks the site of the Mamelon.   Con-
tinuing roughly in a south-westerly direction from
the Malakhoff Hill, the visitor soon arrives at a
large work situated on a spur that runs down towards what was known as our Right Attack, and
which from its size and shape he will at once recog-
nise as the Redan.   The inside of the work has been
cleared and neatly levelled.   There is no trace of the
magazine in the salient, which was blown up by a
chance shell from one of our mortars ; nor of the
one which existed in the north-western angle.
In the centre of the gorge the Russians have
erected a handsome monument, consisting of a
granite obelisk, surmounted by a Russian eagle
wrought in bronze.   Deeply cut into the granite
plinth are two Russian words, which mean, " To
the heroes of the Sorties," which to an Englishman
cannot fail to have a deep significance.   But to the
Russian who reads this simple dedication—and

then gazes across to the hillside where lies the
Graveyard of the Hundred Thousand Dead—could
anything recall the war more vividly ?

About a hundred yards in front of the salient is
a British monument erected to the memory of
those who fell in the storming of the Redan ; and
further on down the spur is a low wall, perhaps as
much as fifty feet long, marking the site of the
Quarries. The ground still bears traces of trenches,
zig-zags, and rifle-pits, the construction of which in
rocky soil and at such short ranges, and in a continuous thunder and lightning storm of shell fire,
must have been a business of consummate difficulty
and danger. The Malakhoff Hill will perhaps be
remembered by the Russians chiefly on account of
the three famous admirals who met their death
there. The Redan, on the other hand, will always
be associated in their minds with the fiercest fighting of the siege, and with the patient and noble
sacrifice of thousands of their best men. It was in
fact the power-house of their defensive system ;
and as much of the active principle as their defence
possessed had its seat and point of issue in the
Redan. The French claim that the immediate
cause of the fall of Sevastopol was their capture of
the Malakhoff ; and in a sense it was so. But,
whilst fully appreciating the fine spirit of the
French assault, it must be borne in mind that
from the moment it began success was practically
assured, because the Malakhoff was a comparatively isolated work as well as being decidedly
weak, whereas the Redan was in the main girdle
of the Russian defences, and was immensely
strong. Moreover, as soon as the last attack on
the Redan was launched, numbers of Russian
soldiers were seen running towards it from the

Malakhoff; and when the French flag was hoisted on the latter work they all ran back again. But it was too late then, and their attempt to turn out the French failed. It is a significant fact that of all the monuments which the Russians have erected in the Crimea, the only one which has been raised especially to commemorate the bravery of the Russian troops is the one in the Redan. The others are either statues to individuals or are intended to mark important sites.

The third day's programme consisted in a visit to the battle-field of Inkerman. The easiest way to get there from Sevastopol is to go up to the harbour by boat to a point midway between Careenage Bay and the mouth of the Tchernaya River, and then walk from there. As, however, I had no means of communicating my wishes to the Russian boatmen, I had to do the whole journey on foot. Starting out along the white and dusty Woronzoff road, I walked until I came to a disused cart-track, leading up on to the high ground known as the Woronzoff Heights; this was probably the remains of a military road constructed to provide lateral communication between our left and right attacks. As soon as the summit of the Woronzoff Heights is gained, a white monument comes into view, in the direction of the Inkerman Heights, by which you are able to set your course. You walk on, and in about half an hour you suddenly come to an enormous ravine with here and there a quarry or a precipice in its steep sides. I seemed to have been suddenly dropped into mountain-battery country— to use an expressive phrase; and then I remembered having read somewhere that the ground at the battle of Inkerman was " unsuited to cavalry." As far as I could fix my position, I was standing a little north of the site of the Lancaster Battery, and the ravine yawning in front of me was the water-course which divides the Victoria Ridge from the Inkerman Heights.   The ground is rocky, and the soil chalky; but the round-backed ridges, so far from being bare, are well carpeted with small grey plants interspersed with poppies and thistles, though there is now but little of the dwarf oak scrub to be seen which at the time of the battle grew there in such abundance.   So thickly indeed was the ground covered with scrub that bodies were found in it weeks after the battle.   The explanation of the disappearance of this characteristic bush is to be found in the fact that fuel was always scarce in the Crimea and that most of it was dug up during the first winter for the sake of the roots, which made good firewood.   There does not appear to be any trace of the windmill that stood near the Guards' camp.   At the north-western end of Mount Inker-man there are three monuments marking the sites of lunettes built during the siege in 1855, when the Russians occupied this ground again ; and on the headland at Cape Troitsky there is now a wireless telegraph station.

Time did not admit of a journey across the peninsula to visit the old town of Kertch, which in 1856 became the headquarters of the Turkish contingent.   This force consisted of four regiments of cavalry, five field and one garrison battery, and sixteen battalions of infantry—all regular Turkish troops under British officers.   The cost of the Turkish contingent was borne by the British Government.   Some of the streets in Kertch acquired strange names ; for example, my father's address was 11 Gentleman Street, but I cannot say by whom this delicate exotic was imported, or how long it survived. With the exception of the battle-field of the Alma, I visited all the fighting grounds in the Crimea, and on the whole they may be said to remain practically unchanged. A few of the once familiar landmarks, such as the wind-mill at Inkerman, have disappeared ; and here and there a monument has sprung into existence. Other legacies of the war, almost as much in evidence as these monuments, are the four large cemeteries containing respectively the English, French, Italian, and Russian dead ; and the new barracks which cover the spur behind the Redan. The country between Sevastopol and Balaclava was possibly a little more cultivated in 1910 than it was in 1854, but the landscape remains the same, the ground wears the same wrinkled expression that it has always worn, and there was still a Black Sea Squadron riding at anchor in the Sevastopol roadstead.

SEVASTOPOL, 1910.

CHAPTER XV

THE PERSIAN GULF IN 1913–14

EARLY in 1913 I was appointed naval and military intelligence officer in the Persian Gulf, in succession to Major G. S. G. Craufurd, Gordon Highlanders, and shortly after my arrival in Bushire I went down to Muscat to call on Rear-Admiral (now Admiral Sir Richard) Peirse, the Commander-in-Chief of the East Indies Squadron, who was paying a visit to that port in H.M.S. *Highflyer*. After a stay of a few days I returned to Bushire in the little old S.S. *Kasara*, the only other European passengers being Mr Hedges of the Indo-European Telegraph Department, and Herr Wassmuss, who was on his way out to officiate as German consul at Bushire. On our arrival we were all sent off to the quarantine station. That afternoon, while we were having tea, Herr Wassmuss turned to me and said :

" What are you doing in the Gulf, Major ? "

" I am a spy," said I.

" So am I," replied the consul, not to be outdone, but somewhat nettled at the unexpected retort.

" Very well," said I ; " then we start fair." There was a long pause, after which Hedges took us out and gave us a lesson in golf on the *mashila*.

Herr Wassmuss was a strongly-built man, of

pleasant appearance, and, though prematurely grey, was full of life and energy. Subtle, astute, insidious, he was a prince of finesse. He spoke English, French, Persian, and Arabic fluently ; and he was a magnificent patriot. But he was no saint. There will be no movement to canonise him after his death. Indeed, I should imagine that the beatification of Wassmuss would lead to something very like a celestial revolution.

I have in my possession an intelligence map of Asia, showing the spheres of activity of the various German and other political agents during the Great War ; printed in large type across southern Persia appears the single word "Wassmuss." For four years he ran the most remarkable one-man show that has ever been put on the political stage. These agents tried hard to get the Persians to exchange their *kullehs* for steel helmets and join the German *jihad*, but it was a situation too well known in the East : they invited a donkey to a wedding, so he said to himself, " What do they want—fuel or water ? "

As soon as the punitive measures in Tangistan had been brought to a conclusion, and the rebellion in Oman checked by the timely arrival of Indian troops, affairs in the Persian Gulf resumed their normal tenor and the gun-runner flitted back into the limelight. Lieutenant-Colonel (now Sir Percy) Cox asked me to go down to Galag, on the Mekran coast, to interview Islam Khan, a gun-running chief whom he had persuaded to come down from Bint. Accordingly I left for Jask, where I embarked in H.M.S. *Fox* and proceeded to the mouth of the Galag creek. I went ashore, and, after a short tramp inland, found Islam Khan in a camp which was surrounded with riflemen " as a

bracelet surrounds the arm." After the *istiqbal*
and the usual exchange of compliments, Islam
Khan proceeded to give assurances of his friendship towards the British Raj, of his future good
behaviour, and all the rest of it, in the most
approved style. However, the interview did
achieve certain results and passed off successfully.
While I was in Islam Khan's camp a violent
southerly wind, or *qaus* as it is called locally,
sprang up, and it was only with the greatest
difficulty that a boat could be got through the
surf to bring me off.

The arms traffic problem in the Gulf was like
a jig-saw puzzle, with pieces scattered about up
and down the Persian and Arab littorals, in Mekran, Fars, Arabistan, and Mesopotamia. We were
gradually retrieving them, but there were still
some missing. During one of my visits to Muhammareh I met two British officers—Captain W. L. S.
Meiklejohn, 106th Pioneers; and Lieutenant C. R. C.
Lane, 19th Lancers—who were studying Persian.
The next time I went there, in December 1913, I
found the Turco-Persian Boundary Commission
in camp about a mile from the British Consulate.
The delegation representing Great Britain in this
undertaking consisted of the following :—Mr A. C.
Wratislaw, British Commissioner ; Captain (now
Sir Arnold) Wilson, Deputy Commissioner ;
Lieutenant-Colonel C. H. D. Ryder, R.E. ; Major
H. M. Cowie, R.E. ; Mr G. E. Hubbard, secretary ;
Captain A. H. Brooke, 18th Lancers ; and Captain
H. W. Pierpoint, I.M.S.

From Muhammareh I went up to Basrah, where
I stayed for some days as the guest of Mr Crow at
the British Consulate. As far as gun-running was
concerned, the centre of interest was not Basrah

itself, but a place called Magil, on the right bank of the Shatt-al-'Arab about four miles above that city. By arrangement with the Turkish Government all materials for the Baghdad railway arriving at Basrah from overseas were dumped here without being examined by the Turkish customs officials. A good many rifles were smuggled ashore with the railway material, and no doubt most of them were used against us in the Great War.

On the 3rd January 1914 I left Basrah in the paddle-steamer *Khalifa*, belonging to Lynch Brothers. It took us five and a half days to traverse the 500 miles between Basrah and Baghdad ; but the journey often used to take longer. It was not an uncommon thing for these steamers to be fired on by the Arabs, and in consequence the bridge was armoured and could be converted into a sort of blockhouse. The funnel of the *Khalifa* contained several bullet-holes.

The extraordinary convolutions of the Tigris can be pictured if one realises that Basrah and Baghdad are not much more than 280 miles apart " as the cock crows." During my visit to Baghdad I stayed at the British Residency as the guest of Colonel and Mrs Erskine. The Residency guard at that time was furnished by the 102nd King Edward's Own Grenadiers, and consisted of an Indian officer and thirty-nine other ranks. The name of the Indian officer was Jemadar Hazari Singh. When war broke out a few months later, they were taken prisoners, and all died in captivity.

On 12th January I was shown over the railway works at Baghdad by the German Engineer-in-Chief, Meissner Pasha, of Hejaz railway fame.

14

Considering how strongly the presence of English-
men, especially British officers, was resented all
along the line at this time, I was agreeably surprised to find Meissner Pasha so communicative.
He made no secret of what was going on. The
whole project seemed to be entirely German,
without any Turkish element at all. Even the
tugs which were bringing up the railway material
from Magil were sent out from Germany. Meissner
Pasha was evidently anxious to get the branch line
from Khanaqin open as soon as possible and to
attract the traffic to this route before the Muham-
mareh-Khurramabad line was constructed. In
the previous October he had made a cursory
inspection of the country between the Persian
frontier and Baghdad, and a regular survey of
this region was now about to be completed. The
Khanaqin branch was to join the main line at
Samaichah. It was confidently expected that the
traffic of the Shi'ah pilgrims between Persia and
Kerbela, and of the Sunni pilgrims between
Baghdad and Samarrah, would ensure these two
lines paying well.

The German intention was to transport the grain
from Mesopotamia to the Mediterranean at Alexandretta, which they declared would rapidly
develop into a vast port and kill Beyrout. As
regards the Gulf section of the Berlin-Byzantium-
Baghdad-Basrah scheme, the terminus was to be
at the last-named city, which would also expand
enormously. As an artery of traffic the railway
would soon supersede the waterway, and would
reduce the mileage between Baghdad and Basrah
to less than three-fifths of what it was by river,
and the time of transit from nearly six days to
fifteen hours. The Tigris is at its lowest, and

therefore navigation is most difficult, during the season of greatest export ; in other words, when the boats have most cargo to carry they are least able to carry it. Thus the railway would score all round, and Lynch's steamers would scarcely be able to remain on the river at all.

In the popular imagination Baghdad is always " the pearl of the Orient," with a pageant of brilliantly robed men, veiled, alluring women, and magnificent camels passing through its gorgeous bazaars. In point of fact its beauty is a good deal exaggerated, whilst the Baghdad camel is generally a very poor creature. Harriet Martineau, in describing the camel, said she considered it the least agreeable brute she knew and that nothing could be uglier, except perhaps the ostrich. To Western eyes the camel is certainly an ungainly animal ; to a son of the desert it is the symbol of beauty. Our word " camel " is merely a corruption of the Arabic *jamal*, which in Egypt is pronounced *gamal*. In Arabic the words for camel and beauty have the same root, the former actually meaning a thing of beauty. It is not because the camel supplies the Arab with transport, clothing, shelter, and food that he admires it, nor even because of the fact that without the camel the desert would be uninhabitable, but because he regards it as in itself a beautiful creature. And surely he is right. Many a time when travelling along the old caravan route between Baghdad and Teheran have I been struck with the beauty of the camel. Strings of these great cattle, as Doughty would call them, with their throats and shoulders covered with black hair so long and thick that you could bury your hands in it ; their headstalls and saddles gay with giant tufts of coloured wool ; all gliding solemnly and, but for the clanging of their bells, noiselessly along, make a picture which, to my mind, fills one with admiration.

During my inspection of the Baghdad railway I met two British officers—Captain R. Meinertz-hagen, Royal Fusiliers ; and Captain G.R. Maitland, 14th Lancers—who were spending their privilege leave in Irak. On my way down the Tigris I stayed a few hours in Kut. Little did I dream that this quiet riverside town would shortly be the talk of the civilised world, or that what nature had withheld in the way of attraction history was soon lavishly to bestow. It may be appropriate at this stage to touch upon the meaning of the term " Kut-al-Amarah," about which there appears to have been some discussion, although the etymology of the name presents no difficulty. The word *kut*, pronounced *coot*, is applied to any permanent habitation or collection of habitations, irrespective of situation. Sometimes it denotes a solitary building, sometimes a walled-in quarter of a town, but in either case it must be defensible. The Amarah constitute the principal division of the Bani Rabi'ah tribe. The name of the town of Amarah lower down the river has no etymological affinity to that of Kut-al-Amarah, and is spelt differently in Arabic.

Just at this time we were watching with great interest, but perhaps too little concern, the political and economic activities of Germany in these regions. There were two outstanding features in the German system : firstly, their merchants were invariably good linguists, highly qualified men, selected with care ; secondly, there was the closest co-operation between these men of trade and their consuls. I have seen a great deal of the correspondence between the German consuls and merchants in the Persian Gulf, and have always been struck by the way in which they worked together. With us it is different. I know a case in which a British merchant submitted a report, containing important political information, to his consul. He received a haughty reply, through which the phrase " His Majesty's representative " ran like a thread of gold, and which concluded impressively with the remark that the British Residency was in possession of full information on the subject at issue. The merchant's letter was duly filed in the Residency, and in the margin of it was written : " I expect we know more about Sheikh —— than Mr —— does." At the beginning of the Great War this same merchant, quite fortuitously, obtained some valuable information, but his first experience had discouraged him, and he did not report it.

The next journey in search of missing pieces of the arms traffic puzzle took me into southern and northern Arabistan, and in March 1914 we set out to visit Ahwaz, Shushter, and Dizful. The expedition was arranged and organised by Major L. B. H. Haworth, the British consul at Muhammareh, and, in order to divest it as far as possible of official character, three ladies—namely, Mrs Haworth, my wife, and Miss Westland—were persuaded to join us. On 25th March we left Muhammareh by river, and reached Ahwaz at daybreak the following morning. Here we parted company for the time being with the consular launch and embarked in the *Shushan*, a small stern-wheel steamer which we found waiting for us above the rapids. We steamed along slowly against the current all day, and tied up for the night at a place called Band-i-Qir, where the two streams, known respectively as

the Gargar and the Shatait into which the Karun
divides at Shushter, unite and are joined by the
Diz, an important tributary of the Karun.   That
evening we reached Shalaili, the highest point on
the Gargar to which steamers can ascend.   From
Shalaili it is about seven miles by road into Shushter.
The next morning we all rode into the town through
scenery which, especially at that time of the year,
is wonderfully picturesque.   Several lines of hills
stretch away into the distance, with a lovely snow-
capped range in the background.   Now and then
the track led us past some rocky ravine where
a small stream was splashing its way down to
the river ; and all round us lay beautiful fields of
opium poppies which lent warmth and colour to the
foreground.   During the forenoon we arrived in
Shushter and established ourselves comfortably
in the house of the consular agent.   We remained
there for three days, sight-seeing and making
investigations.

Shushter is the official capital of northern
Arabistan, and, though interesting, did not strike
us as being a very prosperous town.   Many of
the houses are ruinous and deserted, some being
mere heaps of debris, and the only bridge over the
river is broken.   The appearance of the town
suggests a recent earthquake ; but then, where
would you end if once you began repairing in
Persia ?   The people are quarrelsome, bigoted,
narrow-minded, and intolerant.   They are unfriendly to Europeans and inclined to be fanatical.
They have turned their religion into a barrier
instead of a bridge between themselves and
progress.   To use a phrase which is more convenient than accurate, Shushter is a priest-ridden
place : you could scarcely throw a stone without

hitting a *mujtahid* or a *saiyid*. The inhabitants make rude woollen rugs and felt mats, kullehs, givehs, cloth for abas, copper and German silverware, glazed earthenware, terrifying saddles that would rub any horse or rider—and they manufacture opium. Here you may find the real Persian fireplace, a contrivance for filling a room with smoke and allowing the heat to escape up the chimney. It is in places like Shushter that one comes in contact with quaint characters seemingly reincarnate from the stories of old Persia. Indeed, the town may well have been the setting of the following example :—

One day a religious mendicant went into a fruit-stall, and because the fruiterer did not serve him quickly he abused him. The fruiterer retorted by abusing the mendicant, and the latter becoming very angry struck the fruiterer on the head with his shoe. The fruiterer lodged a complaint against him before the judge. The latter sent for the mendicant and said to him :

" Why didst thou strike this shopkeeper ? " ·The mendicant replied :   " Because he gave abuse unto me."

The judge said to him :   " Thou hast done an evil deed ; but since thou art a poor man I will not punish thee severely. Give half a kran unto this shopkeeper and go thy way."

On hearing this the mendicant took a kran out of his purse and handing it to the judge said : " If such be justice, give thou unto him half a kran." He then struck the judge a terrific welt on the head with his shoe and added :   " Thou mayest keep the other half for thyself."

From Shushter we set out to visit Maidan-i-Naftun, the great oil-fields belonging to the Anglo-

Persian Oil Company. The first day we rode fifteen miles, halting for the night at a rest-house near the hamlet of Abgah ; the next day we made an early start in order to cover the five-and-twenty miles that lay before us. The road was bad and we had to ford a winding stream no less than twenty times before we reached our destination. Through the kindness of our friends we were able to see and to smell a good deal at Maidan-i-Naftun. The gas from the wells is unpleasant and occasionally overpowering ; one effect of it is to turn silver black.

By means of powerful pumps, at a place called Tembi, the oil is forced from the reservoirs near the wells over the watershed beyond the pumping-station, whence it gravitates to the refinery on Abadan Island in the Shatt-al-'Arab.

After visiting these places of interest we returned to Shushter, and on 7th April we started for Dizful. In addition to our own sowars and attendants, and those provided by the consular agent, the Governor of Shushter insisted on sending six mounted *tufangchis* with us, so that altogether we formed quite an imposing caravan. The bridge over the Shatait being in ruins, we had to cross the river on *keleks*, whilst the animals were swum over. It was two or three hours before we were able to start again from the other bank ; but what are two or three hours to a Persian—or to a sitting hen ? Before we had got anywhere near Powinda, where we were to camp for the night, a thunderstorm came on, bringing back to our minds the Persian proverb : " The way is narrow and the night is dark, and the rest-house is far off."

The next day we rode into Dizful, having succeeded in shooting a few chikor and sisi on the way. The chikor in these parts are about the same

size as those of Syria and India, with slight
differences of shade and marking ; they are neither
as plentiful nor as heavy as the chikor to be found
between Kerind and Kermanshah.

The entry of our caravan into this quaint old
Persian city caused some little excitement, as
many of the inhabitants had never seen a white
woman before.   Dizful is a large place, double the
size of Shushter and built on an elevated site which
falls away to the river-bank in conglomerate cliffs
a hundred feet high.   The houses are closely packed,
with the usual flat roofs, and extend along the bank
of the Diz River in a dense, elongated cluster.   The
streets are narrow and crooked, and indescribably
dirty ; so are the majority of its 45,000 inhabitants.
Not long ago an American wrote a book in which
he declared that the Persians were being strangled ;
in Dizful, at any rate, that process would certainly
be easier than asphyxiating them.

The river is spanned by a very old bridge, which
has been broken and clumsily repaired.   Above
this bridge there is a line of mills, quaintly picturesque, running out from the bank into the river.
They are perched on rocks and have artificial
dams ; some are linked together with gangways.

The majority of the inhabitants seemed to be of
a poor type, credulous, ill-favoured, unfriendly,
and with the curiosity of penguins.   Large numbers
of them follow religious vocations.   In the little
booths of the bazaar they make brass and copper
vessels of artistic shapes, samovars, and hand-
painted papier-maché boxes. A curious pro-
fession is that of the *sag-pa*—a man who lets out
watch-dogs on hire.   Caravans for Khurramabad
start from Dizful.   At the time of our visit the
country was looking its best, and consisted of

waving prairies aflame with red poppies. The
town itself is a great place for storks. The Persians
call them *Hajji Lug-lug*, and think it unlucky to kill
one ; just as they think it unlucky to see a hare.
One never seems to get tired of watching storks :
whether they are standing solemnly by their nests
on the house-tops or flying round in stately circles,
there is always something interesting about them.

We left Dizful on 11th April and rode out to the
house of a Persian gentleman, about five miles
away, where we stayed the night. Our host had
a beautiful garden, full of rose, orange, lemon, and
citron trees, and we had dinner on the roof of his
house. It was spring-time and a perfect moonlight
night, and for several hours we sat out under the
stars listening to the enchanting singing of a bulbul,
the bird one reads of so much but hears so little.
That was, indeed, a rare occasion.

The next day we rode to Powinda, where our
caravan had rested on the way up to Dizful ; on
the following evening we got into Shushter after
rather an amusing incident. Our party had tailed
out a good deal, when one of the servants' mules
got loose and galloped off across the desert. This
is, of course, an everyday occurrence when travelling
in Persia ; but someone started the hare that we
had been held up and robbed. One of the servants
immediately galloped on ahead to call in the armed
guard ; but, instead of turning back and coming to
our assistance, they put spurs to their horses and
not one of them drew rein until he reached Shushter.
When they came for their pay the next morning
they remarked, by way of explanation, that they
had gone off to the river to water their horses.
After another short halt in Shushter we started
off down the Gargar on a large *kelek*, a mode of

travelling which we quite enjoyed.   From Shalaili the *Shushan* took us down to Ahwaz : by 20th April we were back again in Muhammareh.

By degrees we found our way back to our head-quarters at Bushire, where we remained through-out the long and trying hot weather.   We were fortunate in having my old friend Lieutenant E. C. Withers (now Commander Withers, C.I.E.), Royal Indian Marine, and his wife, to share our house. Within a mile of us stood the remains of the old fort at Reshire, which was captured by General Stalker in December 1856, after a determined resistance.   A remarkable story is told in con-nection with this exploit.   Shortly before the British troops made their attack, the admiral went ashore to visit General Stalker in his camp. The admiral was provided with a pony, but it happened that he was no horseman, and before long the pony deposited its august burden on the road. The incident provoked a good deal of mirth, but the general's interpreter was much exercised about it.   However, the next day he came to the general and said, with an air of satisfaction : " Sir, I have explained to the people the cause of the admiral's fall yesterday, and have made it all right with them.   I said he was drunk."

When summer was at its height, we were cheered by the announcement that a medal, with a clasp inscribed " Persian Gulf, 1909–14," was to be awarded for the operations in those relentless waters in connection with the suppression of the arms traffic.   Not long afterwards the Austrian Crown Prince was murdered, and within a few weeks of that event half Europe was thundering in war.   The momentous news that Great Britain had resolved to stand by Belgium had scarcely reached us when I received the following remarkable telegram which, were it only on account of the date of its origin, is worth reproducing :—

" *Août* 4.

" *Allemagne a envahi France près Nancy et par Grand Duché Luxembourg. Russie pénêtre Allemagne différents points. Turquie mobilise contre Russie. On dit cent mille Anglais débarqués Belgique. Flotte Allemande embouteillée dans canal Kiel. Cuxhaven et Brême bombardés par flotte Anglaise.*"

CHAPTER XVI

CONSTANTINOPLE IN 1918

IN mid-September 1918 General Franchet d'Esperey, the Commander-in-Chief of the Allied Armies in the Balkans, began a general offensive all along the line, and when I reached Salonika in H.M.S. *Redpole* the battle of Monastir-Doiran was in full swing. We left at once by car for Lake Doiran, and from the Pip ridges, which were covered with fresh signs of battle, watched the beginning of the pursuit to the Strumitsa Valley. The following morning I travelled up to Monastir in the first train that had run into that town for many a day, and there, through the courtesy of General Hanrys, the French commander, we were able to get the latest reports regarding the Serbo-French advance. No sooner had we begun to get a grasp of the general situation than the air became suddenly charged with rumours that the Bulgarians had asked for an armistice. This was signed on September 30th, and so I returned to Mudros.

On 20th October we were all greatly surprised by the arrival in our midst of General Townshend, who had been set at liberty by H.I.M. the Sultan and sent out as an emissary of peace. While at Mudros he received telegraphic instructions from the Chief of the Imperial General Staff to remain where he was for the time being.   Five or six days later a party of Turkish delegates arrived from Constantinople, and on 30th October, through the good offices of General Townshend, the armistice between Great Britain and her allies and Turkey was signed on board H.M.S. *Agamemnon*.

Two days later I was sitting in my little wooden hut wondering where I should be sent now that my amphibious staff appointment had come to an end, when a telegram arrived ordering me to proceed to Constantinople in charge of the first British Mission into Turkey.

In a way our agreement with Turkey constituted rather a quaint document.   Generally speaking the terms were set down in inverse order of import-ance ;   and the first definite step taken by the Allies, namely, the military occupation of Con-stantinople, was not provided for at all.   The case of the Turk, who was led to believe that with the signing of the armistice the situation would begin to clear up, was rather like that of a certain officer of the mercantile marine which actually occurred during the Great War.   His ship had been torpedoed in the Atlantic and the crew picked up by a passing vessel.   No sooner, however, had he got on board than he was torpedoed again.   This time he was rescued by a British destroyer.   On going into the ward-room he found a sheaf of Reuter's telegrams, and the first sentence that caught his eye ran as follows :—" The Admiralty announce that the submarine menace is now well in hand."

The arrangements for our departure were not completed till 6th November, when we left Mudros in H.M.S. *Parthian* and proceeded to Imbros, covering the intervening sixty-four miles in about two hours. Here we were transferred to a small mine-laying vessel in which we made a rough passage to Cape Helles. Off Sedd-el-Bahr we were met by a Turkish gunboat. We followed her carefully through the mine-field, which extended almost up to The Narrows and contained nearly six hundred mines. As we were steaming slowly along, at least a score of these mines must have floated past us. They were huge things with horns, and had presumably broken adrift from their moorings and come to the surface. Soon after entering Turkish waters we passed the famous *River Clyde*, which had played so great a part in the historic landing.

When we reached Chanak the Turkish destroyer which was supposed to meet us there had not arrived, so we disembarked and spent the night as the guests of the Turkish commandant, from whom we obtained a detailed plan of the mine-field. In the early hours of the morning the Turkish destroyer *Basra* arrived. We lost no time in getting on board, and by nine o'clock that evening we were alongside the wharf near the Galata bridge. The Grand Vizier sent cars and representatives to meet us, and as we drove through the crowded streets we were now and then saluted by a German or Austrian soldier, of whom there were about 20,000 in the city, or by some stolid, long-suffering *nefer*, whilst many of the civil population actually cheered. The city was quiet and the people civil and orderly, yet it seemed strange to be moving about amongst the soldiers of nations with whom we were still at war ; it gave one a feeling that is not easy to describe. The Greek community were blatant

and effusive ; they had made an enormous Greek
flag, and were threatening to hoist it on the dome
of Saint Sophia.   Most of the shops were laden
with food-stuffs, though we were told that everyday people were dying in the streets from starvation.   But after all this was natural ; the Greeks
were chattering and the shopkeepers trying to
make money.   So I said to myself : The bride is
at the dressmaker's and the bridegroom at the
jeweller's.   Why are the people talking ?

Comfortable apartments had been reserved for
us in the Pera Palace Hotel, where we remained
for some time as the guests of the Turkish Government.   After dinner, on the night of our arrival,
we went into the large reception room, and as we
entered the orchestra stood up and played *God
Save the King*, whereupon all the German and
Austrian officers and their wives rose and walked
gravely out of the room, whilst some ladies in the
gallery, apparently Greeks and " Sweet Water
Europeans," showered down confetti upon us.
This was the first occasion on which our national
anthem had been played in the Turkish capital
for over four years.

A powerful Benz car, formerly the property of
Enver Pasha, was allotted to me, both the chauffeur
and the attendant being Turkish soldiers.   My
orderly officer was Captain Sedad Bey, a gallant
young cavalryman, who had been severely wounded
at Sari Kamish and had seen much fighting both
in the Caucasus and in Gallipoli.

On the morning after our arrival I went to pay
my official visit to Izzet Pasha, the Grand Vizier
and Minister of War.   He was a big man, of great
personality and charm, and was at the head of a
cabinet which had been formed with the special

object of making as honourable a peace with the Allied Powers as could be arranged. After the usual formalities had been gone through, I explained the object of our mission and informed him that our first cares were the immediate evacuation of all allied prisoners of war and the demobilisation of the Turkish Army. I begged him earnestly to give us his assistance, especially in regard to our prisoners, and I shall never forget his reply. Opening a large gold cigarette case, with a red silk tassel to it, he said to me in French : " We are the vanquished. Have a cigarette, it is all Turkey has to offer you."

The remainder of that day was spent at the Ministry of War, where a spacious office, luxuriously furnished, had been set apart for me, and from the windows of which I could see the *maison rouge*, and watch the *Itfaiye Alai* drilling. Sedad Bey and I sat down and worked out, in feverish haste, a scheme for the evacuation of the prisoners of war, and before the sunset prayer all the telegrams ordering their despatch to various selected centres had been sent out. Everyone of these messages had to be acknowledged by telegraph and the acknowledgment shown to me. In a few days, thanks to the energy of General Javad Pasha, who was Chief of the Staff, the prisoners began to trickle in. This capable and accomplished general became Minister of War in January 1919, but he found the position untenable, and very soon resigned.

On the third evening after my arrival I went out for a drive along the Bosphorus to see the *Goeben*, which was lying at anchor in the little bay at Stenia. She was looking very smart and trim, and was flying a large Turkish flag. I could

15

hardly suppress a feeling of respect for this famous ship which on three separate occasions had completely scored off the allied fleets.

The quiet, orderly behaviour of the Constantinopolitans, both at the time of and after our arrival, impressed us favourably.   One could walk about unarmed anywhere and at all hours.   After dark we frequently heard revolver shots, but they were generally fired by some Greek homeward bound full of money and douzico after a successful evening at the club, and discharging his revolver just to let everyone know he was armed.   But for this, and the weird noise made by the night watchman on his beat, clanging his stick on the stone pavement, all was still.

One day a merchant in Stamboul went round to a friend of his to try and borrow a donkey. When he arrived at the house his friend told him that the donkey was not there as he had just lent it to someone else.   At that moment the donkey began to bray.   " That's strange," said the merchant, " why, I can hear him braying in the yard." " There you are," said the friend ; " you won't believe me, but you believe my donkey."

Some people think that you must expect this sort of logic from a Turk, but that is not the author's experience.   The majority of high Turkish officials are both clever and accomplished and have most agreeable manners.   If the Turks had extended proper treatment to the allied prisoners of war and had abstained from the Armenian massacres they would have come out of the Great War extremely well.   Even those two crimes were the work of individuals, and not of the nation as a whole.

On many occasions at the Ministry of War

Turkish officers impressed upon me the fact that they would rather deal with the British than with any of our Allies. At first I thought this was merely their incorrigible politeness, but it was not so. " All through this war," they would say, " in Egypt, Gallipoli, Mesopotamia, Palestine, Aden, Hejaz, or where you will, we have been fighting against the British. We scarcely met any of your Allies on the battle-field at all. It is the British who beat us and we want to deal with them. We are a nation of soldiers, and is not that what any soldier would say ? " There is no doubt that, at the outset at all events, they were sincere on this point.

One or two of the conditions imposed on the Turks at the signing of the armistice were difficult for them to fulfil, because the necessary organisation did not exist ; yet whenever the Turks attempted to point out their difficulties they were immediately accused of trying to evade the terms of the armistice. The author is convinced that this was not always the case, but still it is very easy to start a cat-call. If a little more courtesy and consideration had been shown them during the first few months after the signing of the armistice, the Allies would not have alienated the sympathies of several persons whose services would have been of great value to them in the settlement of the Turkish question. For example, General Mustafa Kemal, who commanded the Seventh Turkish Army with honour and distinction ; he is now regarded as a bloody assassin, but is really a very good fellow. Within the first three months of our arrival in Constantinople the portfolio of the Minister of War changed hands five times, and the Sultan had some difficulty in getting anyone to accept it.

During the winter of 1918–19 it was not an uncommon thing to see high allied officials visiting Turkish prisons and personally releasing Armenians and Greeks. The Turks at once invested this with a religious character and regarded it, not unnaturally, as a movement against Islam, because whilst great activity was shown in this direction, little or no attempt was being made to arrest those persons who were responsible for the appalling treatment of the Kut garrison, although we had the fullest information concerning the principal offenders. The author actually saw Khalil Pasha walking about the streets of Constantinople at the end of January 1919—that is to say, nearly three months after the arrival of the British. How could this man be absolved from blame ? As commander-in-chief in Mesopotamia and general officer commanding the Sixth Army, it was to him that General Townshend had surrendered ; it was his duty to see that the British and Indian prisoners were treated properly, and in failing to do so he was guilty of criminal neglect. Moreover, it is now definitely known that he connived at, if he did not actually order, the murder of Captain Cowley, of Lynch Brothers, who was awarded the Victoria Cross for his magnificent attempt to run the *Julnar* into Kut.

Life at the Ministry of War was very strenuous, but one Friday morning, finding the great building empty, I voted myself a holiday and went off to see the *Selamlik*. On that occasion this interesting function took place at the Hamidieh Mosque, so I drove to a spot near by from which I could see without being in evidence. Soon after I had taken up my position the Minister of War drove by and unfortunately noticed me. Why I say unfortu-

nately the reader will soon discover. When he
arrived at the mosque he sent his A.D.C. back to ask
me to come up and join him, and though I would
have preferred to remain in hiding I obeyed the
summons. I was ushered into a small room, and
while we were in there drinking coffee and smoking
cigarettes an official entered and announced that
H.I.M. was about to arrive. I tried to escape, but
I found myself being bowed out on to the dais
reserved for the ministers of state. A moment later
the Sultan's carriage came swinging round the
corner, and as it drew up in front of the mosque
the band played the Turkish national anthem. We
all saluted together, but I felt that the imperial
gaze had fallen on me. A solitary staff cap was
not likely to escape notice amongst a small bunch
of *kalpaks*.

The prayers were quickly over, and before a
suitable opportunity of withdrawing gracefully had
presented itself the Sultan sent for me. As none
of the Allies—not even the High Commissioner—
had yet had an audience of H.I.M. this invita-
tion somewhat alarmed me, but I felt it would be
improper to refuse, and I obeyed the summons.
I was shown into a small room adjoining the mosque,
where I found the Sultan seated on a sofa. H.I.M.
Muhammad VI. was a man of distinguished appearance, with a slight figure, a thin and rather sad-
looking face, keen eyes, and a soft gentle voice.
He was dressed in khaki uniform and was wearing
the beautiful diamond insignia of four of his orders.
His Majesty spoke to me in Turkish, and one of
the officers of the household was told off to inter-
pret for me. As I stood there to attention the
Sultan rose and shook hands with me and then
invited me to sit down. Speaking very slowly

the Sultan said : " I am glad to welcome to the shores of my distressful country the son of a man who only knew Turkey as an ally of England." It was a graceful remark and, as I afterwards learned, was expressed in the most elegant language ; but it puzzled me greatly to know how the Sultan had managed to find out that my father had fought on the side of the Turks against their inveterate enemy in the Crimea.   I thanked him for his kind words and added that my father, who had landed in Constantinople with the British and French armies in June 1854, was still alive.   We continued to converse for about twenty minutes when the Sultan remarked : " I understand that you have spent several years in Muhammadan countries ; perhaps it would interest you to see the inside of this mosque." I bowed, whereupon he shook hands with me again, and I withdrew.   I then followed the equerry into the mosque.   Sultan Muhammad VI. of Turkey was the second august personage of whom I had been honoured with a private audience in that memorable year 1918, the other being Pope Benedict XV.   The Great War seemed to have taken away a good deal of the splendour of the *Selamlik*.   On this occasion it was picturesque enough, but it was not the brilliant and imposing ceremony that I remembered witnessing in 1910.

The guards at the Ministry of War were furnished by the Constantinople Fire Brigade, the crack infantry corps of the Turkish Army.   These fine-looking men, in their distinctive uniforms, are very familiar figures in the capital, and Stamboul without its fire brigade would be like Whitehall without the horse guards.   I do not know of a more impressive sight to a soldier than a body of these stolid, determined men, in their red helmets and long grey cloaks, marching with slung arms solemnly through the streets. The Turks call them the *Itfaiye Alai*, or fire-extinguishing regiment, because that is one of their principal duties. When summoned to a fire they turn out very quickly and jog through the crowded thoroughfares at a steady double, calling out *Yangin, yangin*—Fire, fire. If you ask them where the fire is, I believe you generally get a very rude answer.

At the time the armistice was signed Constantinople was full of interesting people, and amongst them was Abbas Hilmi, ex-Khedive of Egypt. In the course of a conversation with the author he admitted quite frankly that he had backed the wrong horse, but he protested that he had good reasons for not wishing to take sides against the Turks. In the first place, he said, he was a Muhammadan with Turkish blood in him ; and secondly, Egypt was under the suzerainty of Turkey, a country in which he owned vast possessions. From his point of view this may have been a strong chain of reasoning, but it did not make him any more desirable as a British ruler.

Another interesting figure was 'Ali Haider, the rightful Grand Sherif of Mecca. His case, as personally explained by him to the author, is a curious one. Many years ago there was some correspondence between his father, who was then Grand Sherif, and the British Government regarding the welfare of a certain political *détenu* at Taif. When it reached the ears of Abdul Hamid, the then Sultan of Turkey, that the Grand Sherif of Mecca had been corresponding with a foreign power, he summoned him to Constantinople and kept him there, the Sherifate passing to the younger branch of the

family.   But for this episode 'Ali Haider, and not
Husain, would now be King of the Hejaz.

The writer had many interesting conversations
with Damad Ferid Pasha, a Turkish nobleman of
great distinction.   I also met Nur-ed-Din Pasha,
whom General Townshend defeated at Ctesiphon.

Amongst the escaped British prisoners who were
still at large in the city were Captain Sir Robert
Paul, Captain A. B. Matthews, and Captain F.
Yeats-Brown.   Then whilst on the subject of
distinguished people one must not forget to mention
Brigadier-General W. H. Deedes, the British
Military Attaché, a man of singular gifts and
charm, a great Turkish scholar, and a born dip-
lomat.   Then there was Miss Whittaker, a
character requiring no introduction to the British
public.

Prices in Constantinople were ruinous, especially
of clothes and boots, and our released prisoners of
war had to pay the most exorbitant rates for
their outfits.   Muhammadan shopkeepers here as
elsewhere have an insidious way of intertwining
religion with business ; they will rant about Allah
and Muhammad and then, like true Propheteers,
ask you sixty liras for a suit of clothes.   Curiously
enough, one of the cheapest articles in Constantinople was a treasury note.   Of course in Turkey
paper money is never worth the corresponding
amount in gold, which latter is at a premium not only
in respect of paper but of silver also.   Small change
too, owing to artificial causes, is at a premium.
In the Ottoman Empire, such is the distrust of
bank and treasury notes of all kinds that on my
arrival in Constantinople in November 1918 I
actually bought some British one-pound notes for
nine shillings each.   If one could have obtained

the necessary gold to have bought up all the British, French, Italian, and Greek notes in the city one could have made an immense fortune.   But the gold was not forthcoming, so that one had to be content with speculating in " ifs " and " ans."

H.M.S. *Superb*,
  February 1919.